Getting it **across2**

One hundred talks for family worship

Nick **Fawcett**

kevin mayhew

First published in 2003 by
KEVIN MAYHEW LTD
Buxhall, Stowmarket, Suffolk IP14 3BW
Email: info@kevinmayhewltd.com

KINGSGATE PUBLISHING INC
1000 Pannell Street, Suite G, Columbia, MO 65201
E-mail: sales@kingsgatepublishing.com

0 1 2 3 4 5 6 7 8 9

ISBN 1 84417 046 2
Catalogue Number 1500577

Cover design by Angela Selfe
Edited by Katherine Laidler
Illustrations by Steve English
Typesetting by Louise Selfe

Printed and bound in Great Britain

Contents

INTRODUCTION   7

ADVENT
1   Prepared for his coming   13
2   Recognising the signs   16
3   Knowing the Bible   18
4   Meeting Jesus   20
5   RSVP   22
6   As white as snow   25

CHRISTMAS
7   A place in our hearts   29
8   What's missing?   31
9   Have I got news for you!   33
10   Sharing the news   34
11   Worth pondering   36
12   A costly Christmas   38

EPIPHANY
13   Seeing the light   41
14   Transforming the ordinary   43

LENT
15   Don't waste it   49
16   Choosing the way   51
17   You decide   56
18   Turning around   58
19   Whose side are you on?   60
20   Recognising our mistakes   62
21   A tempting prospect   64
22   An honest assessment   67
23   Spotting the symptoms   69

PALM SUNDAY
24   The Servant King   73
25   An eternal kingdom   77

HOLY WEEK
26   An amazing price   83
27   Meekness and majesty   85
28   Changing faces   87

EASTER

29 The difference Easter makes   91
30 Easter transformation   94
31 Faith restored   97
32 Telling the news   99

ASCENSION

33 A different dimension   103
34 A glimpse of glory   106

PENTECOST

35 People of the Spirit   111
36 Experiencing the unseen   113
37 Fruit, not flowers   114

TRINITY

38 Beyond comparison?   119
39 A sense of proportion   121

ALL SAINTS' DAY

40 Keeping going   125
41 All saints together   127

NEW YEAR

42 A new chapter   133
43 Looking to the future   135
44 New beginnings   137

WEEK OF PRAYER FOR CHRISTIAN UNITY

45 Working together   141
46 Bound together   144
47 Though we are many   145

MOTHERING SUNDAY

48 Loving hands   151
49 Learning from mothers   156

CHRISTIAN AID WEEK

50 Neighbours   161
51 A raw deal   163
52 Actions speak louder than words   165

FATHER'S DAY

53 Responding to the Father   169
54 The Father of all   174

HARVEST

55	Gifts of the world	179
56	A hidden Harvest message	181
57	Looking into Harvest	183

ONE WORLD WEEK

58	All God's people	187
59	One world	190
60	God's world	192

REMEMBRANCE SUNDAY

61	Let's grow feet!	197
62	Remembering and learning	199

CHURCH ANNIVERSARY

63	Building bricks	205
64	What the Church can become	208
65	Names from the past	212

CHURCH MEMBERSHIP

66	Joined together in Christ	215
67	Belonging together	217
68	Ambassadors for Christ	219

MUSIC/SONGS OF PRAISE SERVICE

69	Make music in your hearts	223
70	Sing to the Lord a new song	226

ORDINARY SUNDAYS

71	Who do you say that I am?	229
72	Seeing things differently	231
73	Foundations	234
74	From small beginnings	235
75	A change of name	238
76	Who created whom?	241
77	A matching picture	243
78	Breaking down the barriers	244
79	Eating together	247
80	Self-centred, God-centred?	250
81	The key to it all	252
82	A God not made with hands	255
83	Honest to God	257
84	Hearing God's call	259
85	A friend in need	260
86	No limits	262

87	That's the limit	264
88	Raising a smile	266
89	A question of faith	267
90	Making whole	269
91	Reshaped!	271
92	Wiping away our tears	272
93	Pulling our weight	274
94	Silent but present	275
95	Spot the difference	276
96	The God who sees in secret	277
97	Setting us free	278
98	The missing piece	281
99	Making it known	283
100	Christian clothing	285

INDEXES
| Subject Index | 289 |
| Index of Main Bible Passages | 291 |

| PHOTOCOPY MASTERS | 293 |

*To Margaret and Ken Turner, in thanks for so many happy
times shared together and for your invaluable support,
friendship and encouragement over the years.*

Introduction

Giving a family talk isn't easy – in fact there are few things harder when it comes to leading public worship. Adults will generally sit politely and hear you out, no matter how boring you are, but a younger audience will have no qualms about making their feelings known. It takes a thick-skinned speaker indeed to plough on regardless when children are fidgeting, yawning, giggling or muttering under their breath, clearly disinterested in everything that is being said. All this perhaps explains why many clergy dispense with a family talk altogether, and why those who do include one frequently pass on the responsibility of preparing it to others within their congregation.

The problem with family talks is that the time and effort involved in preparing them often seems disproportionate to the space they occupy in a service. If we are to avoid being simplistic, patronising or downright dull, we need not only to think of a novel idea that will capture people's imagination but also to develop that idea into a cohesive structure, which usually means creating or collecting a variety of visual aids or other pegs. Understandably, hard-pressed worship leaders frequently conclude that the energy expended in doing this is better used elsewhere. That's where this book comes in. It doesn't do all the work for you – nothing can do that – but it does do most of the spadework, providing guidelines for 100 talks covering the key seasons in the Christian year, significant events in the life of a typical church fellowship, and a variety of ideas for ordinary Sundays. Every talk is set out according to a basic framework. First, I give a Bible passage around which the talk is constructed. This should be read publicly before the talk, unless instructed otherwise. Next, after summarising the aim of each talk, full instructions are given concerning the preparation of visual aids, and, where graphics are recommended, a template – which can be copied and enlarged as required – is supplied in the Photocopy Masters section. Finally, I give suggestions as to how the talk might be delivered, but I would urge you to put this into your own words so that what you say comes across as natural and spontaneous.

So what are the essentials of a family talk? There is no one answer to that, but for me the following are all vital ingredients:

• Keep the talk short and simple

• Include, if possible, an element of fun

• Use appropriate visual aids

• Encourage 'audience' participation

• Ensure there is all-age relevance

- Keep applications (the 'religious' bit) brief
- Prepare thoroughly
- Present things as attractively and professionally as possible

Let me deal with each of these in turn.

Length

The talks in this collection are purposely of varying lengths. Some are suited to a brief slot within a service, to be followed later by a sermon (ideally on the same theme). Others are full-length talks designed to replace the sermon in family services. Whatever the case, avoid waffling or sermonising. Say what you want to say as simply and straightforwardly as possible. Focus on one point rather than attempting to cover many.

Fun

With any audience a little light-heartedness goes a long way towards establishing a rapport. When talking to young people this becomes all the more essential, for there are numerous other attractions in our modern-day society competing for their time. Too often I have attended services in which the 'talk to the children' is little more than a mini (or not so mini!) sermon, the ineffectiveness of this approach eloquently testified to by the scarcely suppressed expressions of boredom. Not only do such talks fail to get the message across – far worse, they effectively drive young people away from our churches.

Visual aids

Some kind of visual aid is generally essential in delivering a successful family talk. What we see stays in our minds far longer than what we simply hear. You may occasionally get away with a straightforward quiz (some of the talks in this book recommend just that), but usually it is worthwhile providing something for people to look at to reinforce the message – even if this is simply key words stuck to a board.

Audience participation

Young people (and many older ones too) like to be involved in a 'learning process' rather than simply being talked to. In my experience, games, word-searches, quizzes and other forms of participation offer an effective way of including the congregation in what you are saying. The last thing children want to feel is that they are back at school.

All-age relevance

As I have said already, many adults are actually far more receptive to a talk geared towards a younger audience than they are to a sermon (many also enjoy participation as much as children, if not more so!). But even if this were not the case, we owe it to any congregation to ensure that a talk is able both to stimulate and challenge.

Brief applications

I have always believed that the secret of a successful family talk is to keep the application (in other words, the serious bit at the end) as short and simple as possible. Ideally, the message you are looking to put across should speak for itself through the illustrations/visual aids you use, though some expansion of what this means is usually necessary. Overdo the application, and you will pay the price. Which of us hasn't witnessed the sudden glazed looks, fits of giggles or uncomfortable fidgeting which somehow spontaneously break out the moment the 'religious' part of a talk is reached. Whatever you do, don't try to ram the point home; if you haven't made the point through the fun part of your talk you won't make it afterwards.

Thorough preparation

Before giving a talk it is well worth running through it at home and checking that you have everything you need. If the talk is built round a word-search, have you checked that all the words are included and spelt correctly? If it involves adding words or letters, do you have these all ready to hand and in the right order? If you are using visual aids, can these be seen clearly by everyone in the church? If you need to make use of a tape recording, is everything plugged in and can the sound be heard at the back of the building? The importance of planning and preparation cannot be overemphasised. The last thing you want is for a talk to grind to a halt halfway through because you have overlooked some vital detail!

Attractive and professional presentation

In our sophisticated technological age people are used to slick, glossy and professional presentations. While we may not emulate these, it is important that any visual material we use be as clear and well presented as possible. The advent of the home computer and the wealth of desktop facilities now at our disposal make such a standard of presentation far easier to achieve than it once was and far less time-consuming. While material can be written out by hand, I would strongly recommend the use of a PC word-processing package if possible, and, better still, some kind of Power-point presentation. When it comes to displaying material, my own preference, arrived at after several years of trial and error, is to use a magnetic whiteboard in conjunction with magnetic tape (available on order through most office stationery suppliers), with the back-up of a second whiteboard (magnetic or otherwise) and blutack. You will also, of course, need easels for these, the lighter you can find the better. A supply of marker pens (in washable and permanent ink) is also a must for many talks, as is a copious supply of thin card and/or paper. Several of the talks could be delivered using an overhead projector and screen if this is preferred to board and easel.

On a purely practical note, make use of a radio microphone if this is available. Family talks invariably involve a degree of movement, and it is all too easy to stray from a standing microphone so that you become inaudible, or to trip headlong over the wires of a halter-neck model (the younger members of the congregation will delight in this, but for you it can prove embarrassing and potentially dangerous).

Summary

Much of the material in this book was first used in public worship during my time as a minister in Cheltenham. Of all the comments received during that time few were more gratifying than those from young people recalling talks I had delivered months or even years earlier. Whether they remembered the point I had been making I cannot say, but whatever else they had enjoyed being in church and carried positive associations of their time there. If we can succeed in doing that, it surely justifies any amount of time and energy expended in 'getting it across'.

NICK FAWCETT

ADVENT

1   Prepared for his coming

Readings   Isaiah 40:1-11; Luke 1:57-79

Aim   To emphasise that the message of Advent is as much about the present – the way we live, think and feel now – as about the future.

Preparation   You will need the following as visual aids: potato peeler, sun cream, recipe book, holiday brochure, GCSE revision book, sandpaper, soap and bowl of water, can of oil, Moses basket, safety glasses/goggles, umbrella, shin pads, cricket gloves or pads.

Talk   Display the items you assembled beforehand, and ask if anyone can identify what they have in common. It is most unlikely that anybody will have a clue. Announce that you have some questions that will help provide the missing link.

1.   Which of the items might you use if you were planning to spend a day on the beach in the middle of summer? (*Sun cream*)

2.   Which might you take if it was going to rain? (*Umbrella*)

3.   Which might you use if you were going to work with machinery? (*Safety glasses/goggles*)

4.   Which might you buy if you or your partner were expecting a baby? (*Moses basket*)

5.   What should you check in your car engine before going on a long journey? (*Oil*)

6.   Which should you use before sitting down for a meal? (*Soap and water*)

7.   Which do you need to use before you start painting a peeling door or windowsill? (*Sandpaper*)

8.   Which would you need to study before sitting an exam? (*GCSE revision book*)

9.   Which might you look at if you're planning to go away on holiday? (*Holiday brochure*)

10.   Which might you need to look at if you're planning a special meal? (*Recipe book*)

11.   Which might you use if you're planning to have chips for lunch? (*Potato peeler*)

12.   Which would you use to plant some potatoes? (*Spade*)

13.   What might you put on before playing a serious game of football? (*Shin pads*)

14.   What might you wear if you're playing a game of cricket? (*Cricket gloves/pads*)

Once all the questions have been answered, ask if anyone has guessed yet what all the items have in common. If people are still unsure, suggest the motto of the Boy Scouts as a clue – 'Be prepared'.

All of the items remind us how important it is to prepare for something in advance. We wouldn't go away on holiday without deciding first where to stay. We wouldn't have much chance of passing an exam if we didn't revise first. We wouldn't make a very good job of decorating if we didn't sand down the area before painting it. We'd risk serious injury playing cricket or football without shin pads or cricket gloves, and similarly if we used machinery without safety glasses. We'd suffer serious sunburn if we lay on a beach without sun cream, and we'd experience a real soaking in a thunderstorm without an umbrella. So often, for a host of reasons, it's vital to prepare for the future, to plan ahead, and that is precisely the message in both our readings today.

First, words spoken three thousand years ago by the prophet Isaiah: 'A voice cries out: "In the wilderness prepare the way of the Lord, make straight in the desert a highway for our God"' (Isaiah 40:3). Isaiah tells the people of Israel to be ready for the coming of the Messiah, the one God is sending to deliver his people, and, almost a thousand years later, those words were to take on new meaning following the birth of a child called John, later to be known as John the Baptist.

> And you, child, will be called the prophet of the Most High; for you will go before the Lord to prepare his ways, to give knowledge of salvation to his people by the forgiveness of their sins. (*Luke 1:76*)

Words spoken by John's father, Zechariah, through which he gave thanks to God that his son was to prepare the way of Jesus. Which, of course, is just what he did, preaching and teaching in the wilderness so that people would be ready to welcome the Messiah when he came.

Here is one of the great truths at the heart of Advent – the fact that God prepared the way for his coming in Christ. Through the words of the prophets centuries back in history, and through so much else in scripture, he revealed his loving purpose so that the world might be ready to welcome him. Yet, as the Apostle John reminds us, many failed to do so, either misreading the signs or preferring their own way to the way of Christ. The coming of Jesus caught them unprepared.

Advent asks us whether we have responded and whether we are any more ready today. Have we listened to God's promises? Have we understood what they mean? Have we opened our lives to his love in Christ? Above all, do we live in such a way that we would be happy to welcome him should he return here and now, or at any moment? No doubt we are all busy preparing for Christmas, buying presents, writing cards, decorating the Christmas tree, planning meals and get-togethers. All of these have their place as part of our celebrations, but Advent asks us, how ready are we to celebrate what this time of year is all about: the birth of Jesus Christ and the new life his coming offers to all?

2 Recognising the signs

Reading

Matthew 11:2-27

Aim

To remind us that there are signs of the coming of God's kingdom, if only we have the faith to believe and a willingness to see.

Preparation

First, reproduce each of the following map symbols on a large sheet of card/paper (one per sheet). Larger versions of these pictures, suitable for enlarging and photocopying, may be found in the Photocopy Masters section on pages 294-295.

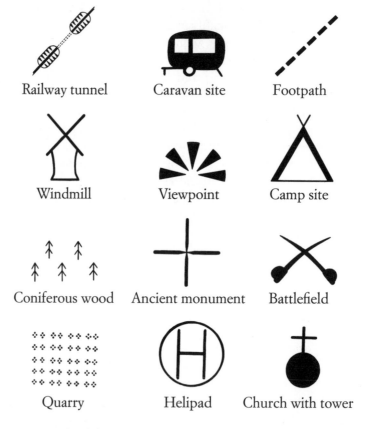

Railway tunnel	Caravan site	Footpath
Windmill	Viewpoint	Camp site
Coniferous wood	Ancient monument	Battlefield
Quarry	Helipad	Church with tower

Have each of the pictures ready to display during the talk.

Talk

Hold up a copy of an Ordnance Survey map and tell the congregation that you want to test their knowledge of the symbols used on maps. One by one, display the pictures you have prepared, asking if anyone can identify what the symbols mean.

Each of these, of course, is only a sign, but all of them point to a reality, and when we have only a map to guide us, then these symbols become vitally important. Interpret them correctly and we will find the way we are looking for; misunderstand them and we will end up hopelessly lost.

John the Baptist began to wonder if he'd misunderstood things, as he lay in prison following his arrest by Herod. He had believed Jesus was the one sent by God to establish his promised kingdom, but now he wasn't so sure, wondering if perhaps he'd misread the signs, so he sent some of his own disciples to question Jesus. The reply they gave set his mind at rest:

> Jesus answered them, 'Go and tell John what you hear and see: the blind receive their sight, the lame walk, the lepers are cleansed, the deaf hear, the dead are raised, and the poor have good news brought to them.' (*Matthew 11:4-5*)

It was all that John needed to know, for here were signs pointing unmistakably to the dawn of God's kingdom.

If Jesus' coming was the dawn, however, the fulfilment of that kingdom is yet to come. Advent reminds us that this fulfilment *will* take place; that Jesus will return to finish what he started and to complete God's purpose. It is easy to get hung up on signs of his coming, on the various portents that may indicate the day is near. Many have done just that, claiming that the last times are upon us, only to be proved wrong. Advent, by contrast, does not call us to focus on the future but instead to live in the present assured that the future is in God's hands. It calls us to look at what God is doing among us, to glimpse the work of Jesus here and now through his Spirit, and to share in that work through our love and witness.

The signs are here all around us, if only we are ready to see. Look at what God has done for you. Look at what he has done for others. Look at what he has done and is doing through Christ, and so trust that his will shall be done and his kingdom come.

3   Knowing the Bible

Readings   Psalm 119:105-112; John 1:14-18

Aim   To bring home that the Bible is not simply a book about the past, but applies to every one of us, every day.

Preparation   Display on a whiteboard or OHP the following riddle so that it can be seen by the entire congregation:

> My first is in BETHLEHEM
> but not in the INN.
> My second's in ISRAEL
> and also in KING.
> My third is in BABY –
> a gift from ABOVE.
> My fourth is in RULER
> and seen in his LOVE.
> My last is in EVERYTHING
> though not seen in FULL.
> The word I am seeking
> applies to us all.

Talk   Tell the congregation that you are going to give various instructions, which you want them to listen to carefully and then to respond as appropriate.

- Anyone with blue eyes, shout 'Me!'
- Anyone born in April, stand up
- Anyone who walked to church, cough loudly
- Anyone 10 or under, wave your left hand
- Anyone aged 11 or over, wave your right hand
- Anyone who's watched *The Lord of the Rings* (you may prefer to substitute a more recently released film), nod your head
- Anyone with two heads, nod them both at once!
- Anyone under five foot tall, wiggle your legs
- Anyone with good hearing, wiggle your ears!
- Anyone with black hair, pat your head
- Anyone who doesn't like cabbage, shake your head
- Anyone whose favourite colour is red, lift both hands in the air
- Anyone born in this town, cheer
- Anyone who's strong, flex your muscles

- Anyone who's feeling hungry, lick your lips
- Anyone who can touch their toes, wink an eye
- Anyone who thinks this quiz is going on for too long, yawn!

Ask how many people responded every time? The answer, of course, is no one. Some of the instructions applied to just a few of us, some to none at all, and some to many, but there was nobody to whom all of them applied. That's not surprising, of course, because we're all different, no two people exactly the same, not even if they're twins.

Take a look, though, at our Advent riddle (display the riddle you prepared beforehand). Can anyone work out the answer? (It is, of course, BIBLE; offer help in solving this, if needed.) Who is the riddle actually about? (*Jesus.*) So why is the riddle about one thing but its answer another? The answer lies in words from our second reading: 'And the Word became flesh and lived among us, and we have seen his glory, the glory as of a father's only son, full of grace and truth' (John 1:14-15a). According to John, what we have here (hold up Bible) is embodied in Jesus. In other words, everything in the Bible is concerned ultimately with him, pointing in some way to his coming, his nature, his calling or his kingdom.

Advent, then, is a time that reminds us of the importance of reading God's word – not just the story of Jesus' birth or simply the Gospels, but all scripture, for through it God speaks not just of the past but of the present and the future; not just to people long ago but to us today. It calls us equally to respond to Jesus, the Word made flesh, the one who came in fulfilment of prophecy and God's promises to bring forgiveness and new life to all. Those too apply as much to you and me today as to those he first came to. Whoever we are, the message of God's coming in Christ applies to us all!

4 Meeting Jesus

Reading

John 20:30-31

Aim

To emphasise that in the Bible, the word of God, we encounter Jesus, the Word made flesh.

Preparation

No advance preparation is needed for this talk.

Talk

- In which book do we meet Man Friday? (*Robinson Crusoe*)
- In which series of books do we meet Piglet, Christopher Robin and Eeyore? (*Winnie the Pooh*)
- In which books do we meet Mr Angry, Mr Happy and Mr Lazy? (*Mr Men*)
- What book tells of the Queen of Hearts, White Rabbit and Mad Hatter? (*Alice's Adventures in Wonderland*)
- In which book do we meet Mowgli, Baloo, and Shere Khan? (*The Jungle Book*)
- In which comic do we meet Dennis the Menace, Minnie the Minx and Roger the Dodger? (*The Beano*)
- In which books do we meet Dick, Julian, Anne, George and Timmy? (*The Enid Blyton 'Famous Five' books*)
- In which books do we encounter Bramwell Brown, Jolly Tall and Ruff? (*The 'Old Bear' books*)
- In which book do we meet Fagin and the Artful Dodger? (*Oliver Twist*)
- In which book do we meet Ratty, Mr Badger and Toad of Toad Hall? (*The Wind in the Willows*)
- In which books do we meet Martha Monkey, Dinah Doll, Mr Plod and Sly the goblin? (*Noddy*)
- In which book do we meet Catherine Earnshaw and Heathcliff? (*Wuthering Heights*)

These are all books in which we meet particular characters, though of course none of them are real, each having been invented by the author. To 'meet' a real person, we need to read an autobiography, a book in which somebody tells the story of his or her life or experiences. Who can identify the authors of the following?

- *Single Minded* (Cliff Richard)
- *Taken on Trust* (Terry Waite)
- *Crying with Laughter* (Bob Monkhouse)
- *Quite Contrary* (Mary Whitehouse)

- *All Creatures Great and Small* (James Herriot)
- *The Downing Street Years* (Margaret Thatcher)
- *My Tune* (Simon Bates)

In these books we encounter and learn something about real people to the point that we feel we know something about them, but, of course, we still don't actually know them any more than they know us.

One book, though, is different, and that's the Bible. In this book there is someone we do not simply come to know about but whom we can know personally: Jesus, the Word made flesh. As the Apostle John puts it at end of his Gospel:

> Jesus did many other signs in the presence of his disciples, which are not written in this book. But these are written so that you may come to believe that Jesus is the Messiah, the Son of God, and that through believing you may have life in his name. *(John 20:30-31)*

5   RSVP

Reading   Mark 1:1-8

Aim   To stress that the most important thing about Christmas is our response, and to show how Mark, through starting his Gospel with the ministry of John the Baptist rather than the Christmas story, brings home this point.

Preparation   Using large letters on a whiteboard or OHP display the following abbreviations:

PTO, SWALK, TTFN, ASAP, OHMS, NIMBY, AWOL, WYSIWYG, AKA, HAND, ATB, BRB, LOL, RSVP

Next – using your own drawings, enlarged cut-outs from old Christmas cards or material from a Christmas clip-art package – prepare the following pictures on large sheets of paper. Display these, together with four blank sheets of paper, around the church.

Angels
Three kings/wise men
Blank sheet of paper
Baby
Shepherds
Single angel (Gabriel)
Blank sheet of paper
Manger
Blank sheet of paper
Bethlehem (idealised silhouette)
Mary (Madonna and child)
Blank sheet of paper
Joseph

Finally, depending on which method you want to use, prime your church organist to play the first lines of the following carols during the talk, or secure a recording of each on tape or CD, ensuring that you are able to skip easily to the first line of each as required. (If you enlist the help of your organist, you will need to plan carefully to ensure that the right piece is played, or silence observed, at the right time during the talk.)

Angels from the realms of glory
We three kings of Orient are
Five seconds of silence!

Unto us a son is born
While shepherds watched
The angel Gabriel from heaven came
Five seconds of silence!
Away in a manger
Five seconds of silence!
Once in royal David's city
The Virgin Mary had a baby boy
Five seconds of silence!
Joseph was an old man

Talk Tell the congregation that you want to start by testing their knowledge of abbreviations. Display the list you prepared earlier, and ask if anyone can identify what each initial stands for.

PTO (Please turn over)
SWALK (Sealed with a loving kiss)
TTFN (Ta ta for now)
ASAP (As soon as possible)
OHMS (On Her Majesty's Service)
NIMBY (Not in my backyard)
AWOL (Absent without leave)
WYSIWYG (What you see is what you get)
AKA (Also known as)
HAND (Have a nice day)
ATB (All the best)
BRB (Be right back)
LOL (Loads of laughs *or* laughing out loud)
RSVP (Répondez s'il vous plait *or* please respond)

What has all this to do with Mark's Gospel? The answer is that each of these says something different, and so does the way that Mark starts his Gospel. Tell the congregation that it's the last of these abbreviations that particularly concerns you, and that you have a second quiz, this time a musical one, that will help explain why. The aim of the quiz is to compare the way Matthew, Mark and Luke open their accounts of the life and ministry of Jesus. (Point out that you have not included John's Gospel because it is unlike the other Gospels, recording several events that they do not mention and approaching things in a slightly different way.) Explain that you (or the organist) will play a musical clue, after which you will call out the name of one of the Gospel writers (see the list on the next page). The aim of the quiz is then to match the tune and Gospel to one of the pictures displayed around the church.

GOSPEL	CLUE	PICTURE
Luke	Angels from the realms of glory	Angels
Matthew	We three kings of Orient are	Three kings/wise men
Mark	**Five seconds of silence!**	Blank sheet of paper
Matthew	Unto us a son is born	Baby
Luke	While shepherds watched	Shepherds
Luke	The angel Gabriel from heaven came	Single angel (Gabriel)
Mark	**Five seconds of silence!**	Blank sheet of paper
Luke	Away in a manger	Manger
Mark	**Five seconds of silence!**	Blank sheet of paper
Luke	Once in royal David's city	Bethlehem (silhouette)
Luke	The virgin Mary had a baby boy	Mary (Madonna and child)
Mark	**Five seconds of silence!**	Blank sheet of paper
Matthew	Joseph was an old man	Joseph

Luke then, tells us about the angel visiting Mary, the birth in a stable and laying of Jesus in a manger; shepherds in the fields and a multitude of angels praising God. Matthew tells us about the angel visiting Joseph, about a child born who will be called God with us, and about wise men bringing their gifts. How about Mark – what does he tell us? The answer, of course, is nothing, yet in another sense he tells us everything, for he starts his Gospel not in Bethlehem or Nazareth but with the preaching of John the Baptist, calling people to turn away from their old life in readiness to welcome the promised Messiah. In doing so he reminds us straight-away of perhaps the most important message of Christmas – that the coming of Jesus into the world calls for a response. In Matthew, the response is from Joseph and the wise men, Joseph accepting Mary as his wife and the wise men journeying from the East to present their gifts. In Luke, the response is from Mary, accepting that with God nothing is impossible. Mark, though, turns the spotlight firmly on the reader – on you and me – asking, through John the Baptist, the simple but vital question: how do we respond to God's coming among us? RSVP!

6   As white as snow

Readings   Psalm 51:1-12; Isaiah 1:12-20; Matthew 1:18-25

Aim   To highlight the transformation that Jesus is able to bring about in our lives.

Preparation   Cut out a picture from a calendar depicting a winter's snow scene. Stick this on to a whiteboard or wall in the church, and cover with a large sheet of blank white paper. Next, copy and enlarge the following shapes (larger versions may be found in the Photocopy Masters section on page 296, or draw your own freehand:

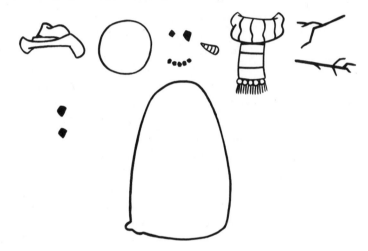

Practise putting these together to form a snowman, as follows:

Fix a piece of blutack to the back of each piece and retain for use during the talk.

Talk   Tell the congregation that you have prepared a picture for them. Point to the blank paper/whiteboard, and ask what they can see? Being winter, it is very possible that someone will suggest it is a snow scene. Announce that you are going to add various pieces to the 'picture' to make things a little clearer. Stick on the various pieces of the snowman, beginning with the body, then the arms, scarf, buttons, head, hat, nose, mouth and eyes, asking each time if anyone can guess what you're making (someone will probably guess early on, if they haven't already done so at the beginning).

Of course, even the heaviest fall of snow doesn't obliterate everything such that all we see is whiteness, as in our original sheet of blank paper, but it does change the way the world looks and feels. (Pull away the sheet of paper, to reveal the winter scene underneath.) No wonder many people feel there's something almost magical about heavy snow, for while it can be both dangerous and a nuisance, it can transform even the most ordinary view into a wonderland, which perhaps explains why both the prophet Isaiah and David in the Psalms used the idea of snow to illustrate the way God's love is able to transform our lives. 'Wash me,' says David in Psalm 51:7, 'and I shall be whiter than snow.' 'Though your sins are like scarlet,' the prophet Isaiah tells us (1:18), 'they shall be like snow.' In other words, however many mistakes we may make, however spoilt our life might be by the things we do wrong, God is able to change us into something beautiful and special, constantly working within us to make us new.

That is a truth at the heart of Advent, with its reminder of the love of God shown in the gift of Christ: the one who 'will save his people from their sins' (Matthew 1:21b). Through him, God accepts us as we are, time and again showing his forgiveness, and through him he helps us to become the people he would have us be. A fall of snow is special, transforming the ordinary into something extraordinary, but the way God in Christ is able to transform lives is more special, more amazing and more wonderful still.

CHRISTMAS

7   A place in our hearts

Readings   Luke 2:1-7; John 1:10-13

Aim   To ask whether we have made room for Jesus in our daily lives.

Preparation In large bold letters, write or print the following, one per page, at
the top of A4-size thick pieces of card:

> JOSEPH, SHEPHERDS, MARY, WISE MEN, HEROD, INN,
> SCRIBES AND PHARISEES, OWN PEOPLE, YOU AND ME?
> (2 copies)

Take another piece of card of the same thickness but a different
colour, and cut out an irregular shape, large enough to write JESUS
in large letters on one side. Make another nine identical copies of
this so that you have ten in all. Take the pieces of card labelled
JOSEPH, SHEPHERDS, MARY, WISE MEN and YOU AND
ME? (first copy), trace around the irregular shape halfway down the
page, positioning it differently each time, and then cut around the
tracing so that the shape fits nicely into the hole, like the last piece
of a jigsaw. Take the pieces of card labelled HEROD, INN,
PRIESTS, OWN PEOPLE and YOU AND ME? (second copy) but
this time cut just inside one or more of the lines so that there is no
way the shape can fit into the resulting space. Rub out any lines that
may be left showing from your original tracing. Stick the 10 pieces
of card, words facing inwards, on whiteboards or any other suitable
vertical surface at the front of the church (making sure you know
where the two cards labelled YOU AND ME? are situated).

Finally, prepare five large red ticks and five large blue crosses (the
mathematical rather than religious kind!).

Talk   Explain that you have prepared 10 'jigsaw' pieces five of which will
fit into the holes on the cards and five of which won't. Ask who
would like to choose one of the cards and try their luck at fitting in
one of the jigsaw pieces. Allow time for volunteers to experiment
with different positions for the jigsaw piece, but if the piece clearly
does not fit step in, say thank you and stick a blue cross (using blutack) over the card. If the piece fits, place a tick over the card.

Continue until every card has either a tick or a cross. Then turn
over the jigsaw pieces and cards except the two labelled YOU AND
ME?, to reveal the significance of the puzzle. The jigsaw piece in
each case represents Jesus, and we see that he found a place in the
heart of Mary, Joseph, the shepherds and wise men; but that there
was no place for him in the heart of Herod or his own people, nor
among the scribes and Pharisees, nor in the inn.

So what of the last two cards: what do they say? Turn these over to reveal the labels YOU AND ME. Here we see simply illustrated the vital challenge of Christmas. Which are we like: those who welcomed Jesus into their lives, joyfully making a place for him, or those in whose lives there was no room? Is there a place in our hearts to receive him?

8 What's missing?

Readings Luke 2:1-16; Matthew 2:1-12

Aim To warn against the danger of losing sight of Jesus as the heart of our Christmas celebrations.

Preparation On a large whiteboard or sheet of paper stuck to a wall, draw the outline of a stable. Then, on A4 sheets of card draw simple outline sketches of the following: angels, three sheep, a star, three wise men, three shepherds, Mary, Joseph, a manger (conspicuously empty), gold, frankincense and myrrh. Position these conspicuously around the walls of the church. Finally, in large letters, print the following on separate strips of card:

> FRANKINCENSE, SHEEP, STAR, WISE MEN, SHEPHERDS, STABLE, MARY, MANGER, JOSEPH, GOLD, ANGELS, MYRRH

Talk Tell the congregation that you want their help in constructing a Christmas nativity mural from the pictures placed around the church. Explain that you are going to read verses from the Christmas stories of Luke and Matthew, each of which will mention something or someone in one or more of the pictures. The first person to put their hand up with the right answer can bring you the matching picture. (If a verse covers more than one picture, allow others to put their hands up once the first volunteer has brought forward a matching picture.) As each picture is brought forward, fasten it with blutack to a large board or piece of paper, gradually building up a simple tableau. Along the edge of the scene, or on a separate board alongside it, place the appropriate word describing the picture (having already positioned the word 'stable'), arranging each as follows:

```
F R A N K I N C E N S E
          S H E E P
      S T A R
          W I S E M E N
            S H E P H E R D S
          S T A B L E
          M A R Y
      M A N G E R
J O S E P H

      G O L D
            A N G E L S
      M Y R R H
```

The Bible verses are as follows:

- Joseph also went from the town of Nazareth in Galilee to Judea, to the city of David called Bethlehem, because he was descended from the house and family of David. (Luke 2:4) – *Joseph*
- He went to be registered with Mary, to whom he was engaged and who was expecting a child. (Luke 2:5) – *Mary*
- And she gave birth to her firstborn son and wrapped him in bands of cloth, and laid him in a manger, because there was no place for them in the inn. (Luke 2:7) – *manger*
- In that region there were shepherds living in the fields, keeping watch over their sheep by night. (Luke 2:8) – *shepherds* and *sheep*
- And suddenly there was with the angel a multitude of the heavenly host, praising God and saying, 'Glory to God in the highest heaven, and on earth peace among those whom he favours!' (Luke 2:13-14) – *angels*
- In the time of King Herod, after Jesus was born in Bethlehem of Judea, wise men from the East came to Jerusalem, asking, 'Where is the child who has been born king of the Jews?' (Matthew 2:1-2a) – *wise men*
- When they had heard the king, they set out; and there, ahead of them, went the star that they had seen at its rising, until it stopped over the place where the child was. When they saw that the star had stopped, they were overwhelmed with joy. (Matthew 2:9-10) – *star*
- Then, opening their treasure-chests, they offered him gifts of gold, frankincense, and myrrh. (Matthew 2:11b) – *gold, frankincense* and *myrrh*

Run through the list of words and nativity scene, pointing out how the pictures you've assembled go together to make up Christmas Day. But do they? Is anything missing? The one thing we've forgotten, of course, is Jesus – the baby in the manger. Sometimes at Christmas we can do just that – leave out the one at its centre, the one who it's actually all about. We turn Christmas into an idealised picture of shepherds and wise men kneeling before the manger, or we forget even about these, seeing it simply as an excuse to have a good time. All these have their place, but all are incidental to what Christmas is finally about: the newborn baby, the Word made flesh, the Saviour, the Son of God. Don't let him be missing from your Christmas.

9   Have I got news for you!

Readings   Isaiah 52:5-10; Luke 2:8-14

Aim   To offer a reminder that the Christmas message applies to us all – it is good news for everyone.

Preparation   Collect a selection of newspapers from the past week and cut out a selection of headline articles concerning topical news items. Ensure that these relate to issues spanning a wide variety of countries, continents or places across the world, and, if possible, choose some that younger children may be able to identify and relate to. Display the headlines, deleting a key word or phrase from each and making a list of the deleted words.

Talk   Tell the congregation that you are going to play your own version of the TV quiz show *Have I Got News for You?* Show the list of words you have deleted from the selection of headlines you have chosen, and then run through the latter one by one, asking each time if anyone can identify the missing word. We read in our newspapers, or hear and see on television, items of news from across the world. Some of those will directly affect us, others perhaps indirectly, but most will have no real bearing on our daily lives, few issues affecting everyone the world over. Our reading today, however, speaks of an event that does just that; an event, of course, that we celebrate once more today: 'I am bringing you good news of great joy for all the people: to you is born this day in the city of David a Saviour, who is the Messiah, the Lord' (Luke 2:10b-11).

Whoever we are and wherever we may be, the message of Christ's birth is, and will always be, good news that can change not only our life but the lives of all those around us – news that still has power to change the world!

10   Sharing the news

Readings   Luke 2:8-18; John 1:6-9

Aim   To emphasise that as well as being news for us (see Talk 9), the message of Christmas is good news for others: news that we have a responsibility to share.

Preparation   Print the following in large bold individual letters so that each can be rearranged afterwards, letter by letter, to form an unjumbled word. Using small pieces of blutack or magnetic tape, display as below on a whiteboard.

HET LAIDY PHARGLEET

TEH EMITS

THE NUS

YADIL LIAM

TEH REXSESP

EHT ARANGDIU

LINNACIAF SMITE

ETH TINNDEEPEND

ILADY RATS

HET ROBVERSE

SAYNUD MOIRRR

RIGMONN TARS

Talk   Tell the congregation that you have jumbled up some newspaper titles. Look at these, one by one; ask if anyone can identify the title.

HET LAIDY PHARGLEET (*The Daily Telegraph*)

TEH EMITS (*The Times*)

THE NUS (*The Sun*)

YADIL LIAM (*Daily Mail*)

TEH REXSESP (*The Express*)

EHT ARANGDIU (*The Guardian*)

LINNACIAF SMITE (*Financial Times*)

ETH TINNDEEPEND (*The Independent*)

ILADY RATS (*Daily Star*)

HET ROBVERSE (*The Observer*)

SAYNUD MOIRRR (*Sunday Mirror*)

RIGMONN TARS (*Morning Star*)

Each of these, with differing degrees of factual accuracy, tells us what's going on in the world around us. They keep us informed of current affairs, both in our own country and further afield. But, of course, not everyone reads newspapers, and in the time when Jesus was born nobody did, for they hadn't been invented then. News in those days was passed by word of mouth, which is precisely what we see in the example of the shepherds. Having been to Bethlehem and seen the child lying in a manger 'they made known what had been told them about this child; and all who heard it were amazed at what the shepherds told them' (Luke 2:17b). The shepherds knew that what had taken place on that night was not simply good news for them but also for all people. Similarly, John the Baptist, whom we heard about in our second reading, proclaimed the good news of Christ, telling all who would listen that here was the Light of the World.

There are some things we can leave to the newspapers, but some things we can't, and one of the latter is the message of the gospel. For one thing, it is no longer seen by the world as news, many imagining they know what it's all about even though they have never heard or responded to that message. Just as important, the picture painted is often twisted and confused, as jumbled as the words we looked at earlier. We need to tell what Jesus means to us, what we have experienced of his love, for there is no substitute for personal testimony, speaking firsthand of what we have seen and know. We have heard again of the 'good news of great joy' for all the people, but as well as hearing it, are we also prepared to share it?

11 Worth pondering

Reading

Luke 2:8-19

Aim

To encourage people to reflect on the Christmas message rather than simply celebrate the occasion and then forget it.

Preparation

Using large letters on a whiteboard or OHP, print the following on one sheet:

Coming home really is sometimes the ideal solution because on rainy nights few other retreats yield options undercover

Each was above nil if the squared area sum approximated for two below the ninth digit

Chewing Tabasco and raw chilli met with impromptu gasps

The important theme unravels or better appears knowable now in hidden text

Talk

Display the first sentence, concealing the rest with a piece of card or paper, and ask if anyone can make sense of it. What is it saying? If nobody spots the hidden message, announce that there is a coded truth concerning Christmas hidden in the sentence. Offer further clues if necessary, though this will almost certainly be unnecessary. The hidden message can be spelt out by taking the first letter of each word in turn, thus making 'Christ is born for you'.

Continue in similar fashion with the next two sentences. By now, the congregation will be alert to what you are doing and should have no trouble spotting the coded messages. In the second sentence this is hidden in the final letter of each word, reading backwards – The word made flesh – and in the third sentence it is hidden in the final letter of each word, but reading forward – 'God with us'. In each sentence there is more than first meets the eye. To anyone prepared to pause and ponder, a whole new meaning appears that wasn't immediately obvious. It's not just in coded sentences that this can be true. We may think we know someone, only to discover hidden depths to their character. We may imagine we have understood something, only to learn new information which forces us to think again. Considered reflection is often needed if we are to see more than just part of the truth.

This, for me, is the truth that emerges from the example of Mary when it comes to Christmas. On the one hand, in our reading, we have the shepherds coming breathless and excited to the stable to see the child the angels told them about, and then rushing out to tell others, leaving them amazed at the good news. On the other hand, we have Mary, who, we read, 'treasured all these words and pondered them in her heart' (Luke 2:19). Did the shepherds and those they spoke to understand the full significance of what had happened? Did they come afterwards to faith in Christ, committing their lives to his service? We do not know, just as we do not know for sure how Mary was later to respond to the life, death and resurrection of her son. What we do know, though, is that in all the trauma, excitement, wonder and mystery of his birth, she made time to stop and think, time to reflect on what it all might mean. And that brings us to the last sentence (display the final sentence and ask if anyone can discover the hidden message – 'think about it' – found through the first letter of each word, but reading backwards.

We do well to learn that lesson in turn, for we can all too easily be so caught up in the fun and festivity of Christmas, even the religious services and celebrations, that we forget to pause quietly and consider what it's all about, what difference it makes to our lives. Enjoy this time and everything that is part of your Christmas, but allow a few moments also each day to consider the events at its heart. Remember that it is about Christ born for you, the Word made flesh, God with us – think about it!

12   A costly Christmas

Reading   Luke 2:25-35

Aim   This talk, particularly suitable for the week after Christmas, aims to bring home the fact that the coming of Christ into the world involved cost as well as reward. It asks if we are ready to make this season a time of giving as well as receiving.

Preparation   On an OHP or whiteboard, display the following riddle in large letters:

My first is in RICHES, and seen in great PRICE.

My second's in JOHN, and heard in his VOICE.

My third is in TREASURES, at least FRANKINCENSE.

My fourth is in GIFTS, and the wise men's PRESENTS.

My fifth is in CHILD as well as in ONLY.

My last is in MARY, found also in HOLY.

My whole is a word that should help us to know

The love God has given, and the love we should show.

Talk   Display the riddle and read it out twice, giving people the opportunity to work out the answer. After allowing a suitable amount of time, ask if anyone has solved it (the answer is COSTLY). Many people may see Christmas as a costly time in the sense of money spent on food, decorations, presents and so forth, but if we look at that first Christmas it involved a different sort of cost. It involved cost to Mary, in allowing herself to be used by God and, as Simeon was to warn her, in subsequent traumas as her son's destiny unfolded. It involved cost to the wise men in the treasures they brought in homage; cost to God in offering his only Son; and cost ultimately to Jesus himself, for he was born to die, to give his life as a ransom for many. Each showed a willingness to give, even to the point of costly sacrifice, and each asks us whether, as well as receiving, *we* are ready to give in turn, ready to accept the cost of discipleship as well as the rewards, ready to take if necessary the path of self-sacrifice and self-denial.

As we share gifts this Christmastime, let us remember how much it cost for Christ to come among us, and let us consider our response to such awesome love.

EPIPHANY

13 Seeing the light

Readings   Matthew 2:1-12; John 1:1-5

Aim   To emphasise that through the coming of Jesus light has dawned in the world, scattering the things that can keep us in darkness.

Preparation   Print the following words in large bold letters and stick them in prominent positions around the church.

STAR, TORCH, LIME, FIRE, SEARCH, DAY, CANDLE, HEAD, SPOT, FLASH, FLOOD, MOON, TRAFFIC, SKY, SUN

Finally, on separate strips of card/paper, print the word LIGHT in large bold print 15 times and arrange in a column down the centre of a whiteboard.

Talk   Tell the congregation that you have prepared a quiz concerning various types of light, and that to help with the answers there are different words scattered around the church, each of which goes with the word 'light'. Read out the clues below one by one, and ask the first person who puts his or her hand up to bring you the word that matches the answer (given afterwards in italics). Stick this on to a whiteboard and place the word LIGHT alongside it.

1. We look up at these as they twinkle in the night sky – *Starlight*
2. Something we might read by under the blankets as children – *Torchlight*
3. Sounds like a luminous fruit, but refers to being the star of the show – *Limelight*
4. Not bright enough to read by, but it certainly keeps you warm – *Firelight*
5. It sounds like we may have to look hard for the answer to this one – *Searchlight*
6. You won't find this during the night, for it's the complete opposite – *Daylight*
7. We perhaps associate this most with Christmas carol services – *Candlelight*
8. You won't get far driving at night without this – *Headlight*
9. Used in the theatre, or as a metaphor for being the centre of attention – *Spotlight*
10. You'll need this if you're taking photographs indoors – *Flashlight*
11. Not used under water, despite how it might sound – *Floodlight*
12. Just the thing, so they say, for a romantic evening stroll – *Moonlight*

13. You'll be in for a fine or may even lose your licence if you jump this – *Traffic light*

14. Not a light, but a window in the roof that lets light in – *Skylight*

15. Without this light, nothing and none of us would be here – *Sunlight*

These are just some of the things associated with light, and each helps give some idea of how important light is to us and how large a part it plays in our lives. Imagine a house in which there were no lights, or a world in which there was no sun! Many find the short days and long nights of winter hard enough to bear, but if there was no light of any sort at any time, we'd all find life impossible.

Epiphany, though, reminds us of a light more powerful and more important than any of these, more special even than the life-giving rays of the sun itself. It is, of course, the light of Christ; a light able to scatter the darkness of evil and death itself, symbolised at Epiphany by the star that guided wise men from the East. 'What has come into being in him was life,' says John (1:3b-5), 'and the life was the light of all people. The light shines in the darkness, and the darkness did not overcome it.' Or, as Jesus himself puts it in John 8:12, 'I am the light of the world. Whoever follows me will never walk in darkness but will have the light of life.'

Epiphany reminds us that however dark life may seem, however gloomy the world may sometimes appear, God's light will continue to shine until that day when darkness is finally fully overcome in his kingdom and there will be 'no need of sun or moon to shine on it, for the glory of God is its light, and its lamp is the Lamb. The nations will walk by its light, and the kings of the earth will bring their glory into it. Its gates will never be shut by day – and there will be no night there' (Revelation 21:23b-25).

14 Transforming the ordinary

Reading

John 2:1-11

Aim

To bring home the Epiphany message that Jesus is able to take what seems ordinary and transform it into something special.

Preparation

This talk takes a fair bit of work, but it's worth it, the visual effect making a lasting impression. It revolves around the ancient art of origami. You will need several A4-size pieces of thin card – any colour will do, although something bold like red may help the 'models' you're going to make stand out better. You will also need some fast-acting glue or sticky tape, a pencil, a pair of scissors, and a long strip (preferably comprising at least 12 connected pages) of computer paper (used paper, if possible, to avoid unnecessary waste). If you want to save on cutting out during the service, you will also need a thick black marker pen. It is worth practising all of the models at home first to make sure they work on the day; otherwise the results could be embarrassing! To avoid people becoming restless, it is important to talk through what you are doing, showing the congregation what's happening at each stage of the model-making.

Talk

Tell the congregation that you've brought along something very ordinary to show them, and hold up your pieces of A4 card. Suggest that what looks ordinary is not, however, always as ordinary as it seems, and then proceed to demonstrate as follows:

Fold one of the pieces of card into quarters and cut one of these out. Fold and then cut this quarter in half lengthways. Take the small rectangle you are left with, and fold this widthways. Your piece of card should now look like this:

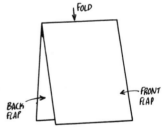

Cut out a notch in the middle of the folded end and trim both edges to make a sort of 'V' shape as illustrated.

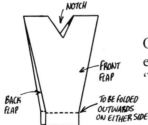

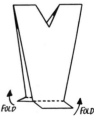

Bend the loose ends outwards on each side, as shown here.

Finally, hold the paper as in the illustration on the left, and, standing close to a microphone, blow hard. The resulting 'whistle' will be well received by youngsters in the congregation and will give any older members who may have dozed off a rude awakening!

A simple whistle, made out of a piece of card. We find the same idea of transforming the ordinary in our reading, though in a much more impressive way. Approached by his mother when supplies of wine run out at a wedding feast, Jesus takes six jars of water and somehow turns them into wine. An astonishing miracle, we might think, but not nearly as astonishing as the truth it symbolises: the fact that Jesus was to transform the life and faith of his nation. And even that is nothing compared to the still greater miracle that Jesus repeatedly performed during his earthly ministry and continues to perform now.

Take a second piece of card and fold it in half and then in half again. Draw a church-window shape in the centre of each segment and door shape at the bottom of one segment and either cut these out or colour them in with a marker pen; then cut crenellations around the top, as follows:

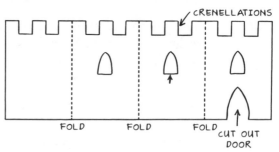

Reverse one of the folds so that the card can then be folded into an oblong shape. Stick down the edges at the top, bottom and centre, as follows:

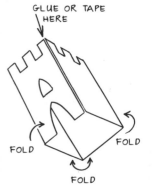

Stand this up lengthways, to make a tower. Take another piece of card and again fold it in half and then in half again, once more reversing one of the folds so that the card can then be folded into an oblong shape. Before making the oblong, however, cut two inches down each crease and fold the resulting flaps in on themselves. Now fold into an oblong, and stick down the edges and flaps as below:

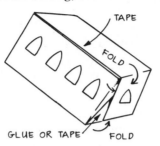

Position the oblong horizontally alongside the tower, as follows:

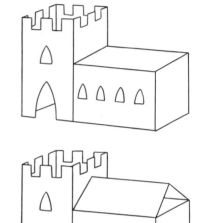

Finally, take another piece of card and fold and cut this in half to form two A5 pieces. Take one of the A5 pieces, and fold it in half lengthways. Cut two inches off one end, then place it over the horizontal oblong, to make a roof. Your model should now look like this.

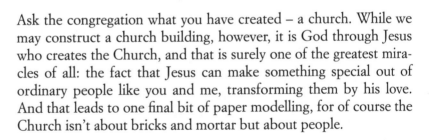

Ask the congregation what you have created – a church. While we may construct a church building, however, it is God through Jesus who creates the Church, and that is surely one of the greatest miracles of all: the fact that Jesus can make something special out of ordinary people like you and me, transforming them by his love. And that leads to one final bit of paper modelling, for of course the Church isn't about bricks and mortar but about people.

Take the computer paper and, keeping the pages joined together, fold each page in half. With the first fold away from you, cut out a half-figure shape, making sure that your cut goes right across to the other side of the paper, as follows:

Ask two volunteers to help you, give them one end of the computer paper each to hold, and gently unravel the 'frieze' you have made, which should look like this:

Again we took what was ordinary and made it into something special, just as God is able to take our lives, take each of us, and use us in a special way, beyond anything we might expect.

LENT

15   Don't waste it

Reading   Luke 12:42-48

Aim   This talk, designed for Shrove Tuesday (so, strictly speaking, outside of Lent), picks up and enlarges on the significance of making pancakes, asking what lessons this tradition might have for us today.

Preparation   Make three pancake shapes out of modelling clay, Plasticene or playdough, and then, using more modelling clay of another colour, mould some letters to spell out RESOURCES, GIFTS and LENT. Press these down (making one word for each) into the 'pancakes'. Place the two 'pancakes' labelled GIFTS and LENT into a large mixing bowl and the one labelled RESOURCES into a frying pan, word facing downwards. Position the mixing bowl and frying pan on a table at the front of the church. Conceal a box of eggs, a pint of milk, a bag of flour, a container of salt and a pat of butter somewhere around the church.

Talk   Depending on the time/day of the service/talk, ask how many people had or will be having pancakes today/this week. Ask if anyone can tell you why pancakes are traditionally eaten on Shrove Tuesday. Explain that pancake-making is a particularly English tradition, originally started to use up stocks of fat, butter and eggs, which, along with meat (not used in pancakes!), were all foods forbidden during the period of Lent, when Christians traditionally fasted to mark the 40 days Jesus fasted in the wilderness before facing temptation. These food items would not keep for 40 days, but poor people particularly couldn't afford to waste precious provisions, so they used them up in the pancakes, enjoying something of a feast in doing so.

In some places, Pancake Day races are still held, such as in the Buckinghamshire town of Olney, where races have taken place ever since 1445, when, so the story goes, a woman was cooking pancakes and, hearing the church shriving-bell summoning people to confession, rushed to church in her apron, still clutching hold of her frying pan.

Ask if anyone can find the ingredients of pancakes that you have hidden around the church. As they are brought forward to you, explain their meaning:

- eggs – symbol of creation
- milk – symbol of purity
- flour – the staff of life
- salt – symbol of wholesomeness
- butter – used as a fat to cook the mixture in.

Tell the congregation that you want to focus particularly on the idea behind pancakes of avoiding waste. Place these 'ingredients' (still in their containers) into the mixing bowl on your table, as you do so place the modelling-clay pancakes labelled GIFTS and LENT on top. Tell the congregation that you are going to make three special pancakes for them, and that you will need three volunteers to toss them for you. Give your first volunteer the frying pan to hold, and ask him or her to toss the 'pancake' inside it. Afterwards, hold this up, revealing the word RESOURCES. Of all the things we cannot afford to waste, resources are perhaps those most often in the news today. We are increasingly coming to realise that supplies of commodities like fuel, minerals, timber and much else are limited and therefore need to be used thoughtfully and wisely, and recycled where possible. As Christians, we have a responsibility to be at the forefront in stewarding this world's resources.

Take the 'pancake' marked GIFTS, place it in the frying pan, and ask a second volunteer to toss it, once again displaying the word on the pancake afterwards. If there's a danger of wasting resources on a global scale, there's equally a danger on an individual level – namely, wasting our gifts. We may be gifted in science or languages, maths or literature, music or graphic design, or perhaps in sport, carpentry or metalwork. Do we make the most of such gifts, developing them to their full potential? Equally, there are gifts in a wider sense: things like health and education. Again, do we make the most of what God has given us?

Ask a third volunteer to toss your final 'pancake', this time revealing the word LENT. Not as many Christians fast today during Lent as was once the case, but many still observe the season in some way. Some make time for prayer or quiet reflection, some meet with Christians of other denominations in study groups, some attempt to kick a bad habit, while others deny themselves certain 'luxuries', giving the money they would have spent to charity or other good causes. Lent marks out 40 days distinct from the rest of the year – once again, we should not waste it.

The simple pancake, as well as providing a tasty meal, has much to teach us. Its lesson is summed up in the last verse of our reading: 'From everyone to whom much has been given, much will be required; and from one to whom much has been entrusted, even more will be demanded' (Luke 12:48). Whatever God gives you, don't waste it.

16   Choosing the way

Reading   Matthew 3:13-4:22; ensure this is read BEFORE the talk.

Aim   To emphasise the importance of choices in life and to explore what might help us in coming to the right decisions.

Preparation   This talk is based on the old TV programme *Blockbusters*. It requires a considerable amount of work, but the enjoyment it gives makes the effort well worth it.

You will need to prepare a grid of hexagons similar to the one below, and to write a different letter of the alphabet in each of the hexagons. I have not used the letters 'x' or 'y', so no questions are provided for these letters. *Blockbusters* used a smaller grid, but this larger size offers scope for more questions.

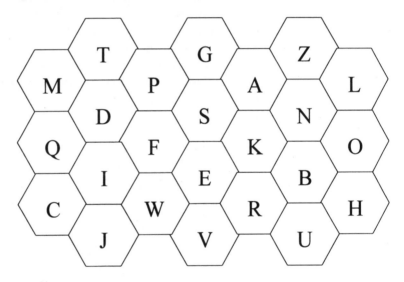

The lettered grid can be prepared in various ways. You might wish to mark it directly on to a whiteboard, you could draw it on a large sheet of card or paper, or you could prepare it on an acetate sheet or computer ready for overhead projection. Alternatively, you could cut out individual hexagons (24 in all) and fix these to a whiteboard using blutack. This takes more time but has the advantage of allowing you to reconfigure the board for a second game. Whichever way you choose, you will need to have some way of highlighting hexagons once a correct answer has been given. Unless you are using some kind of projection method, cut out individual hexagons using pieces of blue and pink card (a different colour for each team/participant). When someone answers correctly, cover the lettered hexagon with the appropriate coloured hexagon. If using the projection method, you will need to shade the hexagon with a piece of coloured acetate, or use 'fill' on a computer.

The original *Blockbusters* is a game for two individuals, but I recommend dividing the congregation into two teams. This is more likely to hold the attention of all and allows everyone the chance to participate. Always ensure, however, that younger people have the chance to answer before older folk leap in.

Talk   Divide the congregation into roughly two halves, telling them that you have devised a game along the lines of the television programme *Blockbusters*. Display the grid you have prepared and explain that the aim of the game is, through correctly answering questions related to today's Bible reading, to turn letters to the colour of your team in a continuous sequence from the top to the bottom of the grid.

The first person to put their hand up (it may be worth enlisting the help of someone to spot each time who this is) will get to answer the question. If a wrong answer is given, the other team have ten seconds to come up with the right one. The answer in each case begins with the letter chosen. Should no correct answer be given, another question beginning with the same letter is asked. When a team answers correctly, it has the choice of the next letter.

Select the blue team to start, and ask them to choose the first letter. A list of questions for each letter of the alphabet is given below (cross out the questions as you go along, to make sure you don't ask the same one twice!). It may be worth having a list of emergency questions, just in case you have need of them.

A

Which 'A' did the Scriptures say would protect Jesus if he jumped off the temple? (ANGELS)

Which 'A' was John the Baptist placed under? (ARREST)

B

Which 'B' did Jesus go through before he went into the wilderness? (BAPTISM)

Which 'B' was Jesus tempted to turn stones into? (BREAD)

C

At which 'C' was Jesus crucified? (CALVARY)

Which 'C' did the way Jesus chose finally lead to? (CROSS)

D

Which 'D' descended on Jesus after his baptism? (DOVE)

Which 'D' tempted Jesus? (DEVIL)

E

Which 'E', meaning the opposite of hard, describes the way Jesus refused to take? (EASY)

Which 'E', the opposite of good, is involved in temptation? (EVIL)

F

Which 'F' is the number of days Jesus spent in the desert? (FORTY)

Which 'F' means to go without food? (FAST)

G

Which place beginning with 'G' was the scene of much of Jesus' ministry both before and after his temptation? (GALILEE)

Which 'G' means the place of the skull? (GOLGOTHA)

H

Which 'H' describes how Jesus felt about 40 days without food? (HUNGER)

Which 'H' was the name of the 'kings' ruling in Judah when Jesus was born and when he was crucified? (HEROD)

I

Which 'I' is the country in which the ministry of Jesus took place? (ISRAEL)

Which 'I's words did Jesus fulfil by going to Capernaum? (ISAIAH)

J

Which 'J' was Jesus baptised in? (JORDAN)

In which 'J' was the temple? (JERUSALEM)

K

Which 'K's did the devil promise Jesus if he would bow down to him? (KINGDOMS)

Which 'K' describes what the devil ask Jesus to do? (KNEEL)

L

Which 'L' is a season recalling the temptation of Jesus? (LENT)

Which 'L' did Jesus bring to those living in darkness? (LIGHT)

M

Which 'M' describes what James and John were doing to their nets when Jesus called them? (MENDING)

Which 'M' did the devil lead Jesus on to? (MOUNTAINTOP)

N

Which 'N' didn't Jesus return to after his temptation? (NAZARETH)

In which 'N' was Capernaum? (NAPHTALI)

O

Which 'O' describes what happened to the heavens after Jesus' baptism? (OPENED)

Which 'O', meaning doing as we are told, did Jesus show in relation to God? (OBEDIENCE)

P

Which 'P' condemned Jesus to be crucified? (PONTIUS PILATE)

Which 'P' did Jesus call to be a disciple? (PETER)

Q

Which 'Q's are we asked during any time of examination? (QUESTIONS)

Which 'Q' means to say what someone else has written? (QUOTE)

R

Which 'R' did John the Baptist call the people to? (REPENTANCE)

Which 'R', the opposite of wrong, was Jesus determined to do? (RIGHT)

S

Which 'S' led Jesus out into the wilderness? (SPIRIT)

Which 'S' was Jesus tempted to turn into bread? (STONES)

T

Which 'T' describes what Jesus faced in the wilderness? (TEMPTATION)

Which 'T' was Jesus tempted to throw himself off? (TEMPLE)

U

Which feeling of 'U' did John the Baptist feel when Jesus asked to be baptised? (UNWORTHINESS)

Which 'U' describes the fire that John the Baptist spoke of? (UNQUENCHABLE)

V

Which 'V' came from heaven after Jesus was baptised? (VOICE)

John called the Pharisees and Sadducees a 'brood of' which 'V'? (VIPERS)

W

Which 'W' was Jesus led into to be tempted? (WILDERNESS)

Which 'W' did the devil want Jesus to kneel and offer to him? (WORSHIP)

Z

Which 'Z' was a land on the other side of the Jordan? (ZEBULUN)

Which 'Z' was the father of James and John? (ZEBEDEE)

Play another game after the first has finished, provided you have enough questions left for a second round. This time, allow the pink team first choice of colour.

The aim of the game is very simple: to make the right choices and then find the right answers that will see you safely through. In each game you have to decide on the best path to take, just as Jesus had to decide out in the wilderness during the time of his temptation. There, at the beginning of his ministry, he had to make choices that would have far-reaching consequences. He had to decide on the right way forward, the path God had chosen for him: whether to live for himself, or live and die for others; whether to seek an earthly kingdom and worldly glory, or to work for God's eternal kingdom, bringing it closer here on earth. The way he chose, of course, was God's way. For us, too, life is full of choices, some of them easy and some difficult. On occasions the right way forward is clear; at other times we must take a step of faith, trusting that we are doing the right thing. The temptation of Jesus, however, offers us guidelines in making those choices. Will we serve our own interests only or consider the needs of others as well? Will we take the way of least resistance or take the path that we know to be right even if it proves costly? Will we follow the way of the world or ask God for guidance, asking what he is saying to us? Will we give in to temptation or resist that which we know to be wrong? Lent reminds us of the need to choose throughout our lives. Which will we follow: our way or God's way?

17   You decide

Readings   Matthew 12:33-37; 1 John 1:5-10

Aim   This talk, like the last, focuses on the importance of choices, but we focus here more on the idea of being responsible for our own decisions and actions. Though God offers guidance, whether or not we follow him is finally down to us.

Preparation   No special preparation is needed for this talk.

Talk   Tell the congregation that you are going to play a simple *Question of Sport* game. (You may wish to divide people into two teams, to introduce a fun competitive element to the talk.) All the questions are concerned with sporting officials and the decisions they might take.

- In what sport might a penalty be awarded for handball? (*Football*)
- What name do we give to the person who makes that decision? (*Referee*)
- In what game might someone be given out stumped/caught behind? (*Cricket*)
- Who makes that decision? (*Umpire*)
- In what sport might a try be awarded? (*Rugby*)
- Who makes that decision? (*Referee*)
- In what sport might the winner squeeze home by a short head? (*Horse-racing*)
- Who makes that decision? (*Steward*)
- In what sport might a false start be called? (*Athletics: track events*)
- Who would make such a call? (*Starter*)
- In what sport might someone call touching ball? (*Snooker*)
- Who makes that decision? (*Referee*)
- In what sport might a points' decision be needed to decide the outcome? (*Boxing*)
- Who makes such a decision? (*Judges*)

These are just a few of the sports people play and the decisions taken within them. In each case a particular official is entrusted with the responsibility of deciding between right and wrong, between what's allowed and what isn't. But let's have a couple more questions:

- In which sport might someone say a club has been grounded in the sand or a wrong ball been played? (*Golf*)
- Who makes that decision? (*The player concerned*)

In golf, as in other sports, there are officials on the course and a tournament referee, but part of the etiquette of the game is that each player acknowledges when they have infringed the rules. There's no arguing with the referee or disputing decisions; if players do something wrong, even inadvertently, they hold their hands up and shoulder the responsibility (as is also true in snooker).

There are parallels in all this with daily life. Sometimes rules are imposed upon us, whether at school or work or simply as citizens bound by the law of this country, and when we break those rules there is someone to reprimand and impose a penalty on us. But there are also times when we must decide for ourselves between right and wrong, and when we must have the courage to admit our mistakes. The time will come, says Jesus, when we are called to account, but it is up to us to decide here and now how we act. No one will force us to take his way, no one will know many of the things we do or think; no one, that is, but us. Are we ready to acknowledge our faults? Do we have the honesty to face up to where we go wrong? No one else can do that for us; *we* must decide.

18   Turning around

Readings Mark 1:1-8; 2 Corinthians 5:16-21

Aim To emphasise that being a Christian involves a constant turning around from our old way of life to new life in Christ.

Preparation Using large letters on a whiteboard or OHP, print the following down the left-hand side of the board/acetate:

LOOT

EVIL

MOOR

DRAWER

FLOG

LEER

REMIT

POOL

TRAP

LIAR

STOP

SNOOPS

STRESSED

REVEL

TRAMS

On separate strips of card/paper, print the words below, attach a piece of blutack, and retain these for use during the talk (if you are using an OHP, you will need to write these on to the acetate during the course of the talk):

TOOL, LIVE, ROOM, REWARD, GOLF, REEL, TIMER, LOOP, PART, RAIL, POTS, SPOONS, DESSERTS, LEVER, SMART

Talk Show the congregation the list of words and ask how many words they can see there? The obvious answer, of course, is 15. Explain that although this is right in one sense, in another sense it is wrong, for these words all have something special about them. Ask if anyone can spot what it is. The answer is that each word can be read backwards as well as forwards. Run through the list, asking if anyone can identify the words reading backwards.

LOOT	TOOL
EVIL	LIVE
MOOR	ROOM
DRAWER	REWARD
FLOG	GOLF
LEER	REEL
REMIT	TIMER
POOL	LOOP
TRAP	PART
LIAR	RAIL
STOP	POTS
SNOOPS	SPOONS
STRESSED	DESSERTS
REVEL	LEVER
TRAMS	SMART

It isn't just words that can be turned round to become something else; today's readings remind us that people can also have their lives turned around in such a way that we can speak of them becoming a different person. That is what John the Baptist was saying as he preached in the wilderness proclaiming the coming of Jesus, and that is what God in Christ has made possible for you, for me and for everyone:

> If anyone is in Christ, there is a new creation: everything old has passed away; see, everything has become new! *(2 Corinthians 5:17)*

Whatever we are, whoever we are, God is always able, through his love, to turn our lives round and make them something completely different, but to do so he needs our willingness to change direction, to follow a new course, to turn each day from the old to the new. Do that, and like these words here our lives will take on new meaning.

19   Whose side are you on?

Readings   Joshua 24:14-28; Colossians 2:6-7

Aim   To emphasise the need for a lasting commitment rather than temporary allegiance to Christ.

Preparation   Given the ever-changing world of football, you may need to update this talk to allow for recent developments in the transfer market. Check that players are still with the clubs indicated and, if necessary, add your own to the list.

Talk   Ask how many people like football. Apologise to those who don't and explain that you have a quiz today about football players and the teams they play for. Ask which sides the following are part of:

- Ryan Giggs   *Manchester United*
- Thierry Henri   *Arsenal*
- Michael Owen   *Liverpool*
- Alan Shearer   *Newcastle United*
- Harry Kewell   *Leeds United*
- Paolo Di Canio   *West Ham United*
- Simon Davies   *Tottenham Hotspur*
- Gianfranco Zola   *Chelsea*
- Kevin Phillips   *Sunderland*

Football fans will have had no problem in identifying which teams these play for, but they will also know that in a season's time it might well be different. Players are often involved with several clubs during the course of their career. They may give their all each time, but with every change of club their loyalties are suddenly switched.

Take the following: what team do the following play for now and what team did they join that club from?

- Nicolas Annelka   *Now Manchester City, formerly Liverpool*
- Rio Ferdinand   *Now Manchester United, formerly Leeds United*
- Jamie Redknapp   *Now Tottenham Hotspur, formerly Liverpool*
- Thor Andre Flo   *Now Sunderland, formerly Rangers*
- Robbie Keane   *Now Tottenham Hotspur, formerly Leeds*
- Richard Wright   *Now Everton, formerly Arsenal*

In football, as in many areas of life, there's nothing wrong with changing direction – for many players it is part of a gradual progression to the top – but in some things, such as family relationships and friendships in general, loyalty is important, and when it comes to serving God, it's essential. That's the message Joshua was emphasising to the people of Israel in our reading:

> If you would rather not serve the Lord, then choose this day whom you will serve, whether the gods your ancestors served in the region beyond the Euphrates or the gods of the Amorites in whose land you are living; but as for me and my household, we will serve the Lord. *(Joshua 24:15, own translation)*

And that's the message Paul was similarly driving home in his letter to the Colossians:

> As you therefore have received Christ Jesus the Lord, continue to live your lives in him, rooted and built up in him and established in the faith, just as you were taught, abounding in thanksgiving. *(Colossians 2:6-7, own translation)*

'Whose side are you on?' says Joshua. 'Keep faithful,' says Paul. Commitment to Christ isn't a five-minute wonder, something we can toy with for a while before moving on to something else. It's about a lifetime's loyalty, staying true through thick and thin, continuing in the faith to the end. Whose side are we on today? More important, whose side will we be on tomorrow, the next day and the next day?

20   Recognising our mistakes

Readings
1 John 1:5-10; 2 Samuel 12:1-7 (*NIV* version – to immediately precede this talk, introduced by urging the congregation to listen especially carefully in readiness for what will follow.)

Aim
To bring home the importance of recognising and acknowledging our mistakes if we are to enjoy a right relationship with God.

Preparation
No special preparation is needed for this talk.

Talk
Ask the congregation how good they are at spotting mistakes. Tell them that you are going to read the first three verses of the reading from 2 Samuel again and ask them to listen very carefully to make sure you get nothing wrong. Read the 'passage' below, keeping as straight a face as possible.

> The BOARD sent TARZAN to JANE. When he came to TIM, he BLED, 'There were two HENS in a certain GOWN, one A FISH and the other A DOOR. The FISH man had a very large number of SHEETS and RATTLES, but the DOOR man had nothing except one little STEWED RAM he had CAUGHT. He BRAISED it, and it FLEW up with him and his PILGRIM. It SHAVED his WOOD, SHRANK from his PUP, and even CREPT in his FARMS. It was like a SAUCER to him.

Ask if anyone spotted something wrong, and then read the passage again, asking people to put their hands up the moment they spot a mistake and to tell you what the correct word should be. The corrected version in full is as follows:

> The LORD sent NATHAN to DAVID. When he came to HIM, he SAID, 'There were two MEN in a certain TOWN, one RICH and the other POOR. The RICH man had a very large number of SHEEP and CATTLE, but the POOR man had nothing except one little EWE LAMB he had BOUGHT. He RAISED it, and it GREW up with him and his CHILDREN. It SHARED his FOOD, DRANK from his CUP, and even SLEPT in his ARMS. It was like a DAUGHTER to him.

These words are part of a parable told by the prophet Nathan aimed at forcing King David to confront the truth and to admit his wrongdoing. He had stolen the wife of Uriah, sending Uriah to his death in order to do so, and until he faced up to that fact, his relationship with God would be forever damaged, a mockery of what it should be. The parable, and subsequent events, had the desired effect, David confessing his sin and seeking God's forgiveness.

The first version was, of course, full of mistakes from start to finish, some of them big, some of them small, but all of them were important for they changed the whole meaning of the reading. Those mistakes were put in deliberately, but when it comes to everyday life there are mistakes that we all make without even being aware of them and that stop us from being the people God wants us to be. Lent is a time for looking honestly at our lives and recognising where we have gone wrong; a time for acknowledging our faults and facing up to our mistakes. Have we the courage to do that?

21   A tempting prospect

Readings   Luke 4:1-13; Hebrews 4:14-16

Aim   To illustrate the fact that temptation is very real, coming in all shapes and sizes, but that God, in Christ, is able to help us withstand it.

Preparation   Copy and enlarge the following drawings on to A4-size pieces of paper or card, and stick them in prominent positions around the church. Larger versions of these pictures may be found in the Photocopy Masters section on pages 297-298.

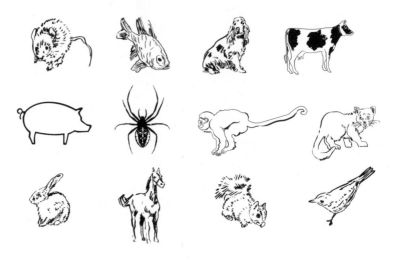

On separate strips of paper/card, print the following in large bold letters and retain for use later in the talk:

BONE, FISH, GRASS, SWILL, MAGGOT, OATS, BANANA, CARROT, NUTS, CHEESE, WORM, FLY

Talk   Our theme today is temptation: what tempts people!

One by one, stick the words you've printed on to a whiteboard, asking what creature might be tempted by the item in question. Invite whoever gives a correct answer to bring the appropriate picture to you. Fasten this to the board next to the relevant word, as follows:

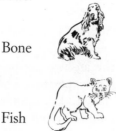

Bone

Fish

Grass

Swill

Maggot

Oats

Banana

Carrot

Nuts

Cheese

Worm

Fly

Each of these items would be an irresistible temptation to the creatures in question. So how about us, what sort of things would we be tempted by? Part of the answer can be seen in the temptation of Jesus. The temptations he experienced have much in common with those that people still face today: the temptation to gain power, to compromise our convictions, to look after number one at the cost of others, and so on. But, of course, those are only some of the things that tempt us. Money, sex, drugs, alcohol are obvious others, but there are many more, most innocent in themselves but capable of leading us astray if taken out of context or pursued to the exclusion of all else. We will face temptation in a host of different forms, and will all fail on countless occasions, so much so that we will sometimes despair of ever serving Christ as we would want to. Lent, though, is a time that urges us not to give up. It reminds us that Jesus was tempted just as we are, so he understands what we are going through and offers help to fight temptation. It reminds us also that if we fail but are genuinely sorry, seeking forgiveness and strength to try again, he is always ready to show grace and mercy; always prepared to put the past behind us and offer a fresh start.

22   An honest assessment

Reading

Romans 5:8

Aim

To emphasise the importance of Lent as a time to look honestly at who and what we are, and then to acknowledge the good and the bad openly to God, seeking his guidance as to how best to use our strengths and overcome our weaknesses.

Preparation

For this talk you will need a large box with a good-size mirror stuck to the bottom of it, facing upwards. For effect, you might also want to have as a prop an empty medicine bottle labelled 'Smelling salts'.

Talk

Gingerly hold up the box you've prepared, and ask if anyone in the congregation is feeling brave. Double-check that they're really feeling confident, gravely warning that you have something truly horrible to show them, so horrible that you barely dare look yourself! Ask volunteers to come forward, but continue to build up the tension, constantly checking that they want go through with the exercise and offering them the chance to sit down again if they wish. Arrange your volunteers in a group to one side, telling them to keep a safe distance, then ask one to come with you to look into the box. Whisper to them not to let on what they see there. Repeat this with each volunteer, asking him or her afterwards how they feel about what they saw? Was it as horrible as they expected? Was it better? Was it worse?

After the last volunteer has looked inside, tell the congregation that it's time they judged for themselves. Walk round the congregation with the box open (or take out and display the mirror). Observe that it was more horrible than anyone probably expected!

Of course, it wasn't actually horrible at all. But what would you say if I had a mirror that was able to show what's going on inside rather than outside, the sort of things we're thinking and feeling? What would we see then, and how pleasant a sight would that be? No doubt there'd be a lot of good things – kind thoughts, fine intentions and so forth – but there would probably also be some not so good things – thoughts, attitudes, intentions that we'd prefer no one to know about.

Thankfully, no one can see what goes on inside our heads – at least no one but God. He sees our best and our worst, our strengths and our weaknesses, the good, the bad and the ugly, and he loves and accepts us as we are – this surely the most important truth at the heart of Lent. Yet that doesn't mean we should sit back complacently, for God is always looking to help us become the people he knows we can be. He wants us to build on our strengths and to overcome those things that separate us from his love. He wants to nurture what is good and to help us conquer whatever prevents us enjoying living life to the full.

To do that means having the courage to look at ourselves honestly, not at the outside but deep within. It means facing up to our faults, acknowledging where we go wrong, recognising where things are not as they should be, and asking God for help and forgiveness. It means being open to the way God might want to use us and open also to the possibility that we have not been as ready as we might be to use our gifts in his service. Are we ready to take a good hard look at ourselves and see ourselves not as we like to imagine but as we really are?

23 Spotting the symptoms

Readings

2 Corinthians 13:5-10; Galatians 5:16-26 (read as part of the talk)

Aim

To bring home the fact that Lent offers a time for us to conduct a thorough self-examination of our spiritual lives, ensuring that our faith is as healthy as it should be.

Preparation

For this talk you can either copy and enlarge (to about A4 size) each picture below or test your own artistic skills! (Larger versions of these pictures may be found in the Photocopy Masters section on pages 299-300.)

Stick the pictures on to a wall or whiteboard.

On separate slips of card/paper, print the following in large bold letters, ready to display underneath the faces during the talk:

CHICKENPOX, FLU, MUMPS, TOOTHACHE, MEASLES, SCARLET FEVER

Talk

Ask if anyone has had a cold recently and what their symptoms were. Ask if anyone has felt so unwell that they've had to consult a doctor. Point to the faces you have drawn and ask what is wrong with each person.

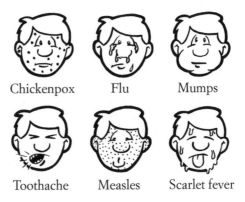

Chickenpox　Flu　Mumps

Toothache　Measles　Scarlet fever

How can we tell what each is suffering from? What clues give their illnesses away? What other symptoms do we associate with these conditions? (Chickenpox: itching and inflamed spots; Flu: sore throat, streaming eyes, sneezing, blocked up or running nose; Measles: high temperature; etc.)

Sometimes we can spot the symptoms of an illness ourselves; at other times we need to consult an expert to find out what's wrong with us. Either way, when we realise something is wrong, we take action, whether it be going to bed, taking medicine, consulting a dentist, or sipping hot lemon.

Most of us recognise the need to look after our physical health, but we can all too easily forget about our spiritual health. Lent calls us to make time for self-examination, to take a long hard look at ourselves so as to judge what sort of shape we are in spiritually. Is our prayer life what it should be? Are our relationships with God and others right? Are we living in the sort of way that God intends, or giving in to temptation, compromising our convictions? As Paul put it in his second letter to the Corinthians, 'Assess yourselves to check that you are living in the faith. Test yourselves to make sure' (13:5a, own translation). Or, in the words of the Psalms, 'Examine me, O God, and search me; test my heart and mind' (Psalm 26:2, own translation).

Lent is a time for a spiritual health check, an opportunity to look honestly at our discipleship and to ask if all is well. None of us is perfect, of course, and the last thing God wants is to encourage a spirit of negative self-criticism. Rather, he wants us to conduct an honest self-appraisal, and then to seek his gracious help in bringing inner healing and renewal. The cure does not lie in us any more than self-help remedies are the answer to every physical ailment. It lies in recognising something is wrong and seeking help from the one who alone is able to give us wholeness. If we are willing to admit our need, he will do the rest.

PALM SUNDAY

24 The Servant King

Readings 2 Samuel 23:1-7; John 18:33-37; John 19:12-16

Aim To contrast the kingship of Christ and the nature of his kingdom with that of earthly kings and rulers.

Preparation No special preparation is needed for this talk.

Talk Ask how many people are good at history. Most people will probably shake their heads, though a few may well be enthusiastic. Explain that you're about to find out, for you have prepared a quiz about various kings, queens and rulers, most, but not all of them, rulers of England. Ask if anyone can identify them from the following clues.

1
Became known as defender of the faith
Led the English church away from Rome
Had six wives
Henry VIII

2
Some say he never actually lived
He had a sword called Excalibur
He is associated with a round table
Arthur

3
The last of the Saxon kings
He was defeated at the battle of Hastings
An arrow in his eye reputedly killed him
King Harold (Godwin)

4
She was a warrior queen
She ruled over the Iceni tribe
She was finally defeated by the Romans
Boudicca or *Boadicea*

5
He was king of Wessex
He was known as 'The Great'
He reputedly burnt the cakes
Alfred (the Great)

6

He originally came from Holland
He married Mary
He sounds like he ruled over a fruit
William III (of Orange)

7

He was also king of Denmark and Norway
He went on a pilgrimage to Rome in 1027
He tried to turn back the sea
Canute

8

He was ruler of England and Scotland during the Great Plague
He married Catherine of Braganza
He became king after the restoration of the monarchy
Charles II

9

He succeeded George V
He married Wallis Simpson
He abdicated shortly after taking the throne
Edward VIII

10

Walter Raleigh was one of her favourites
She was the last of the Tudors
She was queen of England at the time of the Spanish Armada
Elizabeth I

11

He went away on several crusades
He left his brother in charge of the country
He was known as 'The Lionheart'
Richard I

12

She ruled Britain longer than any other monarch
The British Empire was established during her reign
She has an era named after her
Victoria

13

He was known for his personal piety and love of justice
He was king of England during the Battle of Agincourt
A Shakespearean play is named after him
Henry V

14

She was the daughter of George VI
She has the same name as one of our greatest queens
This is the … year of her reign (*enter correct figure*)
Elizabeth II

15

He was the second Stuart King of England and Scotland
The Civil War started during his reign
He was eventually beheaded
Charles I

16

He was king of England from 978 to 1016
Danish raiders took him into exile
It sounds from his nickname that he was caught on the hop
Ethelred the Unready

17

He ruled an ancient civilisation
He was known as 'the Great'
His father, also king of Egypt, had the same name
Ramases II

18

He was eventually forced to commit suicide
He was blamed for the Great Fire of Rome
He was one of the instigators of the persecution of Christians
Nero

19

He was eventually poisoned
He suffered from various physical disabilities and a speech impediment
As emperor of Rome, he annexed Britain to the Roman Empire
Claudius

20

He was the first king of Israel
He suffered from fits of madness
He tried to kill David
Saul

21

He is attributed with writing the book of Proverbs
He was famed for his wisdom
He oversaw the building of the temple in Jerusalem
Solomon

22

He was appointed king by the Romans
His father had ordered all children in and around Bethlehem under the age of 2 to be killed
He was 'ruler' of Israel when Jesus was brought to him for trial
Herod

23

He rode into Jerusalem on a donkey
He was crucified as King of the Jews
He is still worshipped today by Christians as the King of kings and Lord of lords
Jesus

All of these kings, queens and rulers have one thing in common, except the last: they ruled over an earthly kingdom. They did so in different ways, with varying degrees of authority and in very contrasting styles. Some are remembered for their goodness, some are notorious for the mistakes they made or for the sheer evilness of their behaviour, but all would have enjoyed the trappings of state, the power and the prestige that comes with authority; all, that is, except one once again.

The odd one out, of course, is Jesus. He came as king, but his kingdom was not of this world. He came to be crowned, but with a crown of thorns. He came not to serve himself but to serve others. That is the king we honour today: the King of love and Lord of life; the one who offered his life, who gave his all, so that we might share for ever in the joy of his kingdom.

25 An eternal kingdom

Readings Isaiah 9:6-7; Luke 19:36-38; John 18:33-37; 1 Timothy 6:13-16 (all to be read prior to the talk)

Aim This is another talk that makes use of history, but it takes a slightly different tack to the last, contrasting the transience of earthly kingdoms to the eternal kingdom and kingship of Christ.

Preparation In large bold letters, print the following, and arrange them in a column on a whiteboard:

1837-1901

1066-1154

1365-612 BC

1485-1603

500-336 BC

1652-1660

27 BC-AD 476

1550-1070 BC

1558-1603

1154-1422

96-97

1936-1938

1833-1837

613-616

Also print the following:

Isaiah

Luke

John

1 Timothy

Finally, you will need a marker pen to insert a colon in the final four 'dates' of the list.

Talk Tell the congregation that, since it's Palm Sunday, the day on which we remember Jesus entering Jerusalem to be greeted by many as king, you want to think about rulers, kingdoms and empires, and that to help you do this you have prepared some important historical dates for them to consider. Ask if anyone can match the dynasty, empire or era to the appropriate date. The answers are given in italics.

You will need to explain that the Greek and Egyptian empires lasted for thousands of years, with various interruptions and invasions, but that the dates you have chosen are widely recognised as representing the pinnacle of those civilisations. You may also wish, prior to the talk, to print the answers and stick them alongside the relevant dates as each answer is given, even maybe displaying them on the board or around the church beforehand as clues.

1837-1901	*Victorian*
1066-1154	*Normans*
1365-612 BC	*Assyrian empire*
1485-1603	*Tudors*
500-336 BC	*Greek empire (Classical Age)*
1652-1660	*Oliver Cromwell and the Commonwealth*
27 BC-AD 476	*Roman empire*
1550-1070 BC	*Egyptian empire (New Kingdom)*
1558-1603	*Elizabethan*
1154-1422	*Plantagenets*

Each of these represent eras in history where individuals or a succession of people from one dynasty have ruled over a nation or empire, yet all of them, even those dynasties that endured for thousands of years, are consigned to history. So what do you make of the last four entries? (Point to the final 'dates' on the whiteboard. General puzzlement should ensue.)

Give the clue that these are not dates at all. Ask if anyone has any idea what they might be, and indicate that they have already been given a clue in the service. Place the slips of card/paper on which you printed the four names of books of the Bible in front of the four 'dates' and insert colons, as follows:

Isaiah 9:6-9:7

Luke 19:36-38

John 18:33-18:37

1 Timothy 6:13-6:16

The last four entries are in fact Bible verses, but each tells us about a ruler and kingdom unlike any of these. First, there's the prophet Isaiah (9:6-7):

For a child has been born for us, a son given to us; authority rests upon his shoulders; and he is named Wonderful Counsellor, Mighty God, Everlasting Father, Prince of Peace. His authority shall grow continually, and there shall be endless peace for the throne of David and his kingdom. He will establish and uphold it with justice and with righteousness from this time onwards and for evermore. The zeal of the Lord of hosts will do this.

Then there's Luke, and one sentence used particularly of Jesus as he rode into Jerusalem on Palm Sunday (19:38a):

Blessed is the king who comes in the name of the Lord.

Next there's the Gospel of John, and Jesus' words in chapter 18, verse 36, concerning the nature of his kingship and kingdom:

My kingdom is not from this world. If my kingdom were from this world, my followers would be fighting to keep me from being handed over to the Jews. But as it is, my kingdom is not from here.

Finally, there's the first letter of Timothy, and one statement from that reading that says it all (6:14b, 15b):

. . . our Lord Jesus Christ . . . is the blessed and only Sovereign, the King of kings and Lord of lords.

All the other rulers and kingdoms we have considered lasted for a limited span only, each of them now merely dates in history, but with the kingdom of Christ it is different. He came to Jerusalem not to take up an earthly throne but to be raised up on a cross, his kingdom not of this world but beyond death. It is a kingdom many fail to see but one that is inexorably growing among us, each day moving us closer to that time when he will rule for evermore, here on earth as it is in heaven. So we worship him as King of kings and Lord of lords; the one who alone offers an eternal kingdom.

HOLY WEEK

26 An amazing price

Readings Matthew 10:27-31; John 3:16-21

Aim To emphasise that God was willing to pay the ultimate price to overcome everything that keeps us from him.

Preparation Print the following in large bold letters, and display on a whiteboard:

GOLF CLUB	£50	£106,000	£500,000
PLAYING CARDS	£21	£2,555	£99,000
COW	£914,000	£1,245,000	£5,000,100
PIANO	£1,999,999	£1,450,000	£2,300,100
TOY	£2,324	£39,050	£128,333
MEAL	£298.02	£13,091.20	£18,176.07
NUMBER PLATE	£2,000,000	£9,000,000	£15,000,000
PEN	£169,000	£749,000	£1,000,000
HOUSE	£18,000,200	£31,367,400	£62,767,500
WATCH	£8,500	£91,247	£6,820,450
BOTTLE OF WINE	£982	£2,001	£2,435
CHEQUE	£9,999,999	£1,667,500	£2,474,655,000

Talk Begin the talk by holding a light-hearted auction for charity (auction something simple, like a homemade cake, hand-knitted scarf or suchlike). See how high the congregation are willing to go in their bidding.

Afterwards, explain that you are going to play an unusual version of the TV show *The Price is Right*. Each of the items in question was sold for what was then a world record, but can anyone guess the price? Run through the list of items on your display board, displaying the name of the item and the three prices on the board. Below is the correct price, together with additional information.

- GOLF CLUB: A Scottish putter was sold for £106,000 and is now on display at Valderrama Golf Club in Spain
- PLAYING CARDS: A pack of playing cards was sold to the Metropolitan Museum of Art in New York for £99,000
- COW: A Friesian cow was bought at auction in Vermont for £914,000
- PIANO: A Steinway piano once belonging to John Lennon was bought by George Michael for £1,450,000
- TOY: An antique toy hosepipe was sold at auction in New York for £128,333
- Meal: A meal for three at Le Gavroche in London cost £13,091.20

- CAR NUMBER PLATE: In 1994 a car number plate was sold in Hong Kong for £9,000,000
- PEN: A pen made in Switzerland and called 'La Modernista Diamonds' was sold in London for £169,000
- HOUSE: In 1997 a house was sold in Hong Kong for £62,767,500
- WATCH: A watch costing £6,820,450 was sold at auction in New York
- BOTTLE OF WINE: A bottle of 1993 Beaujolais Nouveau was sold at auction in the same year for £982
- CHEQUE: The largest cheque ever written was by Glaxo plc to the Wellcome Trust, for £2,474,655,000

In all of the above we are talking about astonishing amounts of money, a price that some people were willing to pay but that most of us wouldn't even dream of. Yet even the highest figure that we can think of is as nothing compared to the price that God was willing to pay to redeem us; a price that is spelt out in the Gospel of John (3:16, own translation): 'God loved the world so deeply that he gave his only Son, so that anyone who believes in him will not die but will enjoy everlasting life.' Why did he do this? Because we are good, deserving, worthy? No, the answer is in the words of Jesus recorded in Matthew (10:29-31, own translation): 'Are not a couple of sparrows sold for one pence? Yet not even a single bird will fall to the ground without your Father noticing. Believe me, he has numbered even the hairs of your head. Don't be frightened, then; you are more precious than many sparrows.' That's why God was willing to pay the ultimate price, ready to offer his own Son for the life of the world, because each one of us is of infinite value to him, unique and precious, someone to be treasured. Unworthy we may be; in his eyes we are nonetheless of limitless worth.

The figures we have talked of today, and the items they were spent on, are truly astonishing, but the fact that God was willing to give so much for those as undeserving as us is more astonishing and more marvellous still!

27 Meekness and majesty

Reading

Mark 15:16-39

Aim

To illustrate how in the death of Christ on the cross we glimpse both his meekness and majesty.

Preparation

Print the following in large bold letters:

BLOOD, CROWN, THORNS, CROSS, NAILS, HANDS, FEET, THIEVES, FORGIVE, DIE, SPEAR, SON OF GOD, LOVE, GRACE, MEEKNESS, MAJESTY

Cut out each letter and attach magnetic tape to the back, and then arrange on a board as follows:

S	L	O	V	E	M	C	R	O	S	S
O	F	D	I	E	E	F	E	E	T	T
N	O	M	A	J	E	S	T	Y	T	H
O	R	H	C	N	K	S	B	G	H	I
F	G	A	R	A	N	P	L	R	O	E
G	I	N	O	I	E	E	O	A	R	V
O	V	D	W	L	S	A	O	C	N	E
D	E	S	N	S	S	R	D	E	S	S

Talk

Explain that you want to think about the meaning of the cross, and, in particular, about the words used in the Graham Kendrick hymn, *Meekness and majesty*. Ask if anyone can answer the following questions, each of which is found somewhere on the display board. As each correct answer is given, remove the letters from the grid and rearrange them at the bottom of the board.

1. What did Jesus say he would shed as he shared wine at the Last Supper? (his BLOOD)
2. What did the soldiers place on to Jesus' head? (CROWN of THORNS)
3. What was Jesus made to carry before being crucified on it? (CROSS)
4. What did the soldiers hammer into Jesus? (NAILS)
5. Where did they hammer them? (HANDS and FEET)

6. Who were crucified either side of Jesus? (THIEVES)

7. What did Jesus ask God to do to his enemies? (FORGIVE)

8. What did Jesus do after he cried out 'It is finished'? (DIE)

9. What did the soldiers thrust into his side to make sure that Jesus was dead? (SPEAR)

10. Who did the centurion at the foot of the cross say Jesus was? (SON OF GOD)

11. What did Jesus say we can show no greater example of than in laying down our life for our friends? (LOVE)

12. What 'amazing' thing do we see in the fact that Jesus died for us? (GRACE)

Your display board should now look like this:

```
                    M

                    E

    M   A   J   E   S   T   Y

                    K

                    N

                    E

                    S

                    S
```

BLOOD CROWN THORNS CROSS NAILS HANDS FEET THIEVES FORGIVE DIE SPEAR SON GOD LOVE GRACE

The two words left are, of course, MEEKNESS and MAJESTY, and it is no accident that we can arrange those in the form of a cross, for both of them are seen so powerfully in the death of Jesus. On the one hand, we see there the one who accepted a crown of thorns rather than an earthly kingdom, the one who was crucified alongside thieves, allowing nails to be driven into his hands and feet, the one who was ready to die for us, shedding his blood as the spear was thrust into his side. For those, though, with eyes to see, here was the Son of God, the King of love, and the most wonderful example of the grace of God. Here was God and man, suffering servant and crucified Saviour, the one who died so that we might live. Meekness and majesty: two sides of the one Lord, revealed so graphically in the cross.

28   Changing faces

Reading   Various Bible verses are included as part of this talk.

Aim   To explore the changing emotions underlying Holy Week (from Palm Sunday through to Easter Day), and to illustrate that God is with us even in times of confusion, sorrow, despair and fear, able to restore faith, joy, hope and trust.

Preparation   In large bold letters, print the following verses and stick them on a whiteboard or in conspicuous positions around the church.

> Jesus said, 'Now my soul is troubled.' (*John 12:27*)
>
> They . . . fled from the tomb, for terror and amazement had seized them. (*Mark 16:8*)
>
> The whole multitude of the Disciples began to praise God joyfully. (*Luke 19:37*)
>
> His disciples did not understand these things at first. (*John 12:16*)
>
> He denied Jesus again, angrily. (*Matthew 26:72*)
>
> He found the disciples asleep, weary through sorrow. (*Luke 22:45*)
>
> Jesus said, 'Do not let your hearts be troubled, and do not let them be afraid.' (*John 14:27b*)

On separate pieces of paper, print the following: Confused, Sad, Amazed, Troubled, Overjoyed, Angry, Afraid. Fold up the pieces of paper ready to distribute among volunteers during the talk.

Talk   Ask the congregation how good they are at pulling faces. Invite seven of the young people to come forward to have a go. Hand out the words on the pieces of paper you prepared prior to the talk, one per volunteer. Ask each volunteer to pull a face expressing the named emotion and then take a poll of the congregation each time to see whether they can guess what face is being pulled. Ask each time if someone can spot a verse matching the expression (the matching pairs are given below).

> Jesus said, 'Now my soul is troubled.' (John 12:27) – *Troubled*
>
> They . . . fled from the tomb, for terror and amazement had seized them. (Mark 16:8) – *Amazed*
>
> The whole multitude of the disciples began to praise God joyfully. (Luke 19:37) – *Overjoyed*
>
> His disciples did not understand these things at first. (John 12:16) – *Confused*
>
> He denied Jesus again, angrily. (Matthew 26:72) – *Angry*

He found the disciples asleep, weary through sorrow. (Luke 22:45) – *Sad*

Jesus said, 'Do not let your hearts be troubled, and do not let them be afraid' (John 14:27b) – *Afraid*

Our mood and feelings can change just as easily as our faces, as Holy Week so powerfully reminds us. One moment, as Jesus rode into Jerusalem, the crowd were overjoyed, celebrating and praising God, welcoming him as God's promised Messiah; the next, they were angrily shouting 'Crucify!' 'We have no king but Caesar!' One moment, the disciples were professing undying loyalty; the next they had scattered to save their skin, Peter angrily denying he had ever known Jesus. One moment they were looking to the future full of hope; the next, they saw cause only for fear; joy, faith and confidence giving way to sorrow, fear and confusion. Even Jesus himself experienced the trauma of emotional turmoil in the Garden of Gethsemane as he faced up to the prospect of death.

Yet the emotions of Good Friday were to be transformed once again in the days that followed, as the risen Christ appeared first to Mary and then to his disciples. Doubt and confusion were replaced by faith, sorrow by joy, despair by hope and fear by confidence. They realised that even in their darkest hour, God had been there, identifying with them and working out his purpose.

There is the truth at the heart of Holy Week: that the suffering, evil and darkness which had seemed victorious was not some ghastly mistake but woven into God's purpose, death paving the way to new life for all. Whatever we may experience, remember that ours is a God always at work and able to transform each and every situation, however hopeless it may seem.

EASTER

29   The difference Easter makes

Readings   John 20:1-29; Galatians 1:13, 22-23

Aim   To emphasise the transforming power of God's love, supremely shown in the resurrection of Christ.

Preparation   Copy, enlarge and cut out the following pictures of the tomb of Jesus, and print on the back of each in large bold letters DOUBT and FAITH respectively. (Larger versions of these pictures may be found in the Photocopy Masters section on page 301.)

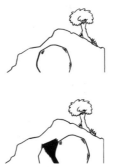

Using pieces of sturdy card, cut out four large long thin rectangles, two vertical and two horizontal, the latter slightly smaller than the others. In as large letters as possible, write out the following words on the back of the rectangles, as follows:

J O Y L O V E V I C T O R Y	E N D D E A T H H A T R E D

DESPAIR   SORROW   DEFEAT

HOPE   BEGINNING   LIFE

Next, copy and enlarge the two pictures below and stick these on to two separate boards.

Finally, using small pieces of blutack, stick on the rectangles (arranged into the shape of a cross, words facing downwards), and the tomb shapes, to make two separate 'tableaux', one a 'scene' of Calvary and the other of the empty tomb. (NB. The Calvary scene uses the 'End, Death, Hatred' and 'Despair, Sorrow, Defeat' cross pieces, and the empty tomb scene uses the 'Joy, Love, Victory' and 'Hope, Beginning, Life' cross pieces.)

Larger versions of the pictures may be found in the Photocopy Masters section on pages 302-303.

Talk

Display the two pictures you have prepared and tell the congregation that one represents Good Friday and the other Easter Day. Ask if anyone can spot the differences between them (eight in all: extra figure in first picture, no sunshine in first picture, extra cloud in first picture, extra birds in second picture, grass missing in second picture, stones missing in second picture, different markings on left-hand cross in second picture and of course the stone rolled away from tomb in second picture).

There are eight differences that we can see almost immediately, though of course the only differences we are actually told of are that it was dark on Good Friday with the stone rolled against the tomb, but light on Easter Day and with the stone rolled away. There are, though, other important differences between Good Friday and Easter. Let me show you what those are. (Turn over the central cross and the tomb in each picture and then stick these back in position so that the words are showing.)

After the death of Jesus, the cross must have symbolised all the things in the first picture: a place where hatred had triumphed over love, despair over hope, sorrow over joy, death over life; a place of defeat where all his followers' dreams had come to an end, faith in consequence giving way to doubt. But on Easter Day all that changed, for they came to realise that Jesus was risen and alive, the cross not what they had imagined after all but used by God in the fulfilment of his purpose. Far from the way things had seemed, love had triumphed over hatred, hope over despair, joy over sorrow, life over death; the cross a place of victory – and all at once faith was reborn.

That's what we celebrate today: the glorious message of the empty tomb and the wonderful truth that in the suffering and agony of the cross God was supremely at work.

30   Easter transformation

Reading   John 20:1-29

Aim   This talk, like the last, focuses on the way Easter turns around not just death but every aspect of life.

Preparation   On separate squares of thin card, one per letter, print the following:

TROUBLE

HOPELESS

FRIGHTENED

CONFUSED

UPSET

AFRAID

SCARRED

DISPIRITED

STUNNED

ALL ALONE

BEATEN

Attach small pieces of magnetic tape or blutack to the back of each letter, and keep the set of letters for each word separate, ready for use later in the talk.

Talk   Tell the congregation that you want to compare the feelings of the Apostles and followers of Jesus in the time immediately after his death and then following his resurrection. To do so, you have two 'quizzes' for them: the first concerned with the former feelings and the second concerned with the latter. Read out the following clues, inviting people to guess the answer (offer prompts, if necessary) and as each correct (or more-or-less correct) answer is given, arrange the letters on a whiteboard, to spell the word out (arrange these words in a column down the left side of the board):

- Something we get into as children when we're naughty *TROUBLE*
- The word describing a situation where there seems to be no future *HOPELESS*
- Another word for scared *FRIGHTENED*
- Another word for puzzled *CONFUSED*
- May mean we're sad or in tears, or that something's been spilt *UPSET*
- Another word for scared and frightened *AFRAID*

- We are this when we have a mark left by a physical or emotional injury *SCARRED*
- A word meaning having lost heart or lost enthusiasm *DISPIRITED*
- We may be left feeling this by a physical or emotional blow *STUNNED*
- Two words meaning that we're totally abandoned *ALL ALONE*
- A word meaning that we've lost a contest or been thrashed by someone *BEATEN*

All of those words describe how the followers of Jesus felt following the death and burial of Jesus. They were frightened, upset and confused, stunned by what they had seen and left feeling all alone in a hostile world. They believed Jesus and everything he stood for had been beaten, and they were afraid of what trouble they might face as a result. Understandably, they felt scarred and dispirited by their experience, all their dreams having apparently been crushed.

But all of this is to reckon without the miracle of Easter and the glorious message of resurrection; a resurrection that was to extend into every aspect of their lives. To help illustrate the transformation Easter brought, consider the following clues. (As each correct answer is given this time, remove the letters you need from the words on display, and make a fresh column of new words on the right-hand side of the board. At the end, all the letters should have been reused.)

- Jesus told Nicodemus that we need to be this if we would be Christians *REBORN*
- This means being sure of yourself or without any doubts *CONFIDENT*
- Another word for happy or overjoyed *DELIGHTED*
- A word meaning confident, guaranteed or in no doubt *ASSURED*
- Another word for sure *CERTAIN*
- A word meaning enthused or brilliant *INSPIRED*
- Another word for brave, daring or courageous *FEARLESS*
- This means promising or optimistic *HOPEFUL*
- Another word for amazed or astonished *ASTOUNDED*
- A word meaning positive, optimistic or looking on the bright side *UPBEAT*
- Two words meaning prepared or ready to go *ALL SET*

The words we had before have totally gone, having given way to words with a completely different meaning. As they discovered the empty tomb and then met with the risen Lord, the followers of Jesus were delighted and astounded, suddenly hopeful, upbeat and confident about the future. Faith was reborn, so that they felt certain he would be with them, assured of his guidance whatever they might face. The days that followed were to see those who had been frightened and hesitant turned into fearless and inspired disciples, all set to do whatever was asked of them.

The transformation could hardly have been more complete, and it is a transformation that God goes on making in all those who respond to Christ, resurrection taking place each moment of every day in their lives. The message of Easter is not just about the disciples or others, but also about what God has done for us.

31 Faith restored

Reading

Luke 24:13-35

Aim

To bring home the fact that resurrection involves not only life after death but renewal in every area of life.

Preparation

In very large letters, print the word FAITH and stick it to a piece of thick card. Cut the card into a simple jigsaw of 15-20 pieces. Affix segments of magnetic tape to the back of each puzzle piece (if you do not have a magnetic board, use blutack when it comes to reassembling the broken jigsaw later in the talk), then make up the jigsaw on a large non-magnetic board and lay this on a table in the church.

Talk

Tell the congregation that you have been busy making a jigsaw that you very much want to show them. Pick up the board as if to hold the puzzle up and clumsily allow the puzzle to slip off and crash to the floor, where, hopefully, the pieces will come apart (if they don't, then separate them as you stoop down to pick the puzzle up). Express consternation, and ask for help in putting the puzzle back together again. Enlist the help of a couple of volunteers, and rebuild the puzzle to reveal the word FAITH.

The jigsaw puzzle, of course, is a simple one, but the word it reveals, and the way we've rebuilt it, carries an important message, for, just as the puzzle was broken into pieces, so too was the faith of the Apostles as they witnessed the agony and death of Jesus on the cross. They had followed him for three years, slowly coming to recognise him as the Messiah, and they had expected, somehow or other, for Jesus to ride into Jerusalem and establish God's kingdom, but instead they had seen him arrested, mocked, flogged and tortured. For all of them it had been a crushing blow, and as Jesus was laid in the tomb so their hopes and faith were buried with him.

That's what we see in the two disciples walking home along the Emmaus Road. 'We had hoped that he was the one to redeem Israel,' they say of Jesus to the stranger who suddenly joins them. Such hopes, though, had been cruelly crushed as they watched Jesus die on the cross, and now, even though they have heard from the women who went to anoint his body that the tomb is empty they refuse to believe it. Their faith lies in pieces, like their shattered dreams. Until, that is, they stop and break bread with this man who has joined them, and afterwards light dawns, hope returns, faith is reborn as they realise that he was none other than Jesus, alive as the women had said, risen just as he had promised before his death.

At that moment, they too came alive again, life transformed, the future full of promise and the present given new meaning. They knew then, as they would know for the rest of their lives, that resurrection not only gave them hope of life to come but new life then and there, restored and reborn every day. That is the truth of Easter that we in turn celebrate today. Thanks be to God!

32 Telling the news

Reading   Matthew 28:1-20

Aim   To emphasise that the good news of Easter is something we are called to share.

Preparation   Record on videotape brief excerpts of television newsreaders (about 15 excerpts, if possible). Set up a television and video in the church that can be clearly seen by all, and ensure that the video is rewound to the beginning of the first excerpt. Double-check everything is working smoothly to make sure you are not caught short in the talk. (If organising a television facility is difficult, this talk could be successfully given using an audio recording only.)

Talk   Play the video clips, asking the congregation to identify each newsreader. These are all people whose job it is to read the news. We rely on them to tell us what's going on, to keep us informed, to make sure that we're aware of anything important happening around us.

Though we may not have the makings of a newsreader, there's a sense in which we're all called to do the same, as the words of our reading make clear: 'Go, then,' says Jesus, 'and make disciples of all people, baptising them in the name of the Father, the Son and the Holy Spirit.'

Do people recognise us as those who have something important to share, as those who tell the news?

ASCENSION

33   A different dimension

Readings   Luke 24:50-53

Aim   To show that the Ascension was the final catalyst in helping the Apostles to grasp the true nature of Jesus, it fully revealing his glory.

Preparation   Using large letters on a whiteboard or OHP, print the following:

A   B   ...   D   E

$101 + 11 = ...$

MCL =

40 pence x 6 = ...

MICE

Talk   Tell the congregation that you have some absurdly simple questions that you want their help in answering. Ask the following, one by one, pointing to the whiteboard where appropriate, and express astonishment each time someone gives you the 'correct' answer, pronouncing it incorrect instead. Build up the congregation's mood of puzzlement as you go through, appearing to become increasingly incredulous at the wrong answers suggested.

- What's missing from the following? A B ... D E? *(Refer to whiteboard)*
  The natural but 'incorrect' answer is 'C'.
- What is the answer to the following? 101 + 11 *(Refer to whiteboard)*
  The natural but 'incorrect' answer is 112.
- What does MCL mean? *(Refer to whiteboard)*
  The natural but 'incorrect' answer is 1150.
- What year is it?
  The natural but 'incorrect' answer is the year in which you are giving this talk.
- What is the capital of this country?
  The natural but 'incorrect' answer is 'London'.
- How many books are there in the Bible?
  The natural but 'incorrect' answer is 66.
- What time is it?
  The natural but 'incorrect' answer is the exact time you ask the question.
- How much is the following? *(Refer to whiteboard)*
  The natural but 'incorrect' answer is £2.40.
- What fuel do most cars use?
  The natural but 'incorrect' answer is 'petrol'.

- Where would you find Birmingham?
  The natural but 'incorrect' answer is in the Midlands of the UK.
- What is Elizabeth Taylor famous for?
  The natural but 'incorrect' answer is 'for being a film actress'.
- How many yards are there in a mile?
  The natural but 'incorrect' answer is 1760.
- What does the word 'piano' mean?
  The natural but 'incorrect' answer is 'a musical instrument'.
- Where would you find Washington?
  The natural but 'incorrect' answer is 'in the USA'.
- What are MICE? *(Refer to whiteboard)*
  The natural but 'incorrect' answer is 'small rodents'.

At the end of the 'quiz', ask who's feeling confused. Then, go through the questions again, this time giving the following 'correct' answers.

- What's missing from A B ... D E?
  G (gamma) if following the Greek alphabet.
- What is the answer to 101 + 11 = ...?
  8 if using binary numbers.
- What does MCL mean?
  It's an abbreviation meaning Master of Civil Law.
- What year is it?
  According to the Jewish calendar, it's 3762 years later than the current year according to the Gregorian calendar.
- What is the capital of this country?
  In Roman times, the capital was Colchester.
- How many books are there in the Bible?
  The Roman Catholic Bible has 73 books.
- What time is it?
  In Sydney, Australia, the time is 14 hours earlier than here (i.e. add ten hours to find the correct time).
- How much is 40 pence x 6
  In pre-decimalised money it makes £1.
- What fuel do most cars use?
  According to the Americans, most cars run on gas (or gasoline)!
- Where would you find Birmingham?
  There's a place called Birmingham in Alabama in the USA.
- What is Elizabeth Taylor famous for?
  Elizabeth Taylor (1912-1974) was a British novelist born in Reading.
- How many yards are there in a mile?
  There are 2025 yards in a nautical mile.
- What does the word 'piano' mean?
  The word piano in a musical score means 'softly'.

- Where would you find Washington?
  There's a place called Washington in northeast England.
- What are MICE?
  MICE are engineers; that is to say, Member of the Institution of Civil Engineers.

You can see that all the answers you gave, just like all those I've given you, are both right and wrong. Birmingham *is* in the Midlands, there *are* 1760 yards in a mile, 101 + 11 *does* equal 112, MICE *are* rodents, C *is* the third letter of the alphabet, and so on. Each of the questions can be looked at in two different ways, and the answer we give depends on how we approach it.

The same is true of so much of life. There is often more to something than meets the eye, as the disciples slowly came to learn was the case with Jesus. At the beginning of his ministry, when he first called them to follow him, they probably saw him as little more than a gifted teacher and preacher; someone special, certainly, but not, as they later came to see him, the Son of God. Even when Peter made his celebrated confession of faith in Jesus as the Messiah, what he meant by the term was very different to what Jesus meant. When Jesus rode into Jerusalem on Palm Sunday, his followers still expected him to claim political authority and an earthly kingdom. So when they saw him instead nailed to a cross it must have seemed that everything they had believed was wrong, a terrible and tragic mistake. Even after he rose again they didn't fully grasp who he was and what it meant. Their faith was constantly growing as they looked behind Jesus' humanity to his divinity, as they glimpsed God behind the man. And in the mysterious event of Ascension, in whatever it was that happened on that day, they came to realise as never before that he was both one with them yet one with God. He was a king, but his kingdom was not of this world. He came to bring new life, but life of a different quality and dimension. He had died, but death was not the end. The cross, which had seemed a place of defeat, was in fact the place of victory!

On the day of Ascension, the disciples finally realised that they had been giving the wrong answer because they had failed to understand the question; they had looked for one meaning when Jesus had been pointing to another.

What of us? Have we glimpsed the full wonder of what God has done for us in Christ? Do we recognise his living presence with us now? Are we awake to the signs of his kingdom all around? Ascension reminds us that Jesus is greater than we can ever begin to imagine; that he offers a new dimension to life, a different perspective to each day, and a fuller experience of God's Sovereign power, awesome love and unfailing grace.

34   A glimpse of glory

Readings   Mark 16:1-14; Acts 1:6-11; John 1:14

Aim   To emphasise that just as the disciples only gradually came to grasp the full glory of Jesus, so our understanding of who he is and what he has done should be constantly growing.

Preparation   On a piece of card (ideally, of good thickness and several feet across), write out the word GLORY, using as large letters as space permits. Cut out these letters, so that you have letter-shaped holes in the card. Cover these holes over from behind with pieces of coloured tracing paper or crepe paper (for added effect, use overlapping pieces to cover each letter, thus creating a mosaic/stained-glass window appearance). Next, cover over the front of the letters with thick pieces of card, three pieces to each letter, fitted together so that they do not overlap. Use blutack for this so that each piece can be easily removed as questions are answered during the service. The pieces of card need to have the following initials written on them, one initial/set on each:

P

B

C

S

P

N E

L J G

N A

J B B

R

M

T

N A

H C

P, J and J

When you have finished preparing this display, position it in a prominent position at the front of the church, preferably at eye level, and set up two or three desk lamps behind it to create a back-lighter effect shining through the letters once the pieces of card covering them are removed.

Talk Tell the congregation that you have something very special to show them at the front of the church but that to see it they need first to answer some questions. Pointing to the appropriate initial/s, ask the following questions, removing the appropriate initialled card once a right answer is given and thus slowly revealing the word GLORY underneath:

1. Which bird beginning with P gives a glorious display by raising its tail feathers? *Peacock*

2. Which B begins as a humble caterpillar but emerges in a glorious new form from a chrysalis? *Butterfly*

3. Which C exchanged her rags to go to the ball in glorious style until midnight? *Cinderella*

4. Which small white flower beginning with S gives a glorious display for a few weeks early each year? *Snowdrop*

5. Which bird of ancient mythology beginning with P was said to rise gloriously from its ashes? *Phoenix*

6. Which part of America, beginning N E, is celebrated for its glorious autumn colours? *New England*

7. Which L J G enjoyed the glory of being Queen of England for nine fleeting days? *Lady Jane Grey*

8. In which N A do we find the words 'happy and glorious, long to reign over us'? *National Anthem*

9. Which song, with the initials J B B, has a chorus that begins, 'Glory, glory, hallelujah'? *John Brown's body*

10. Which great empire, beginning with R, reached as far into Britain as Hadrian's Wall but now leaves only a few traces of its former glory? *Roman*

11. Which M came down off Mount Sinai with his face radiating the glory of God? *Moses*

12. Which glorious ship, beginning with T, sank on its maiden voyage? *Titanic*

13. Which N A experienced his moment of glory as the first person to walk on the moon? *Neil Armstrong*

14. What glorious sight can be seen in the sky every 76 years? *Halley's Comet*

15. Who glimpsed the glory of Jesus at his so-called transfiguration? *Peter, James and John*

Ask the congregation what word has been revealed. The answer, of course, is GLORY, and the more questions we asked, so the more glory shone through until it could be fully seen. But what sort of glory are we talking about? Our questions were concerned with brief moments of glory associated with certain individuals, creatures, plants or objects, but such glory is a short-lived thing, here today and gone tomorrow.

Our readings point to a different sort of glory: the glory of Christ. It was glimpsed first by Peter, James and John in the mysterious event known as the transfiguration. High up on a mountaintop they came to recognise Jesus as the fulfilment of the law and the prophets, the promised Messiah, reflecting God's glory as Moses had done on Mount Sinai centuries before. Yet if this was a glimpse of glory, the full picture was only to emerge later, as, following his death and resurrection, Jesus was taken from their sight and they realised as never before that he was not just sent *by* God but was one *with* him, sharing his glory. So John writes in his Gospel (1:14):

> And the Word became flesh and lived among us, and we have seen his glory, the glory as of a father's only son, full of grace and truth.

Was this the end of story? No, it was only the beginning, for it meant that there was always more to understand; the full wonder of Christ, as with the wonder of God, something that we can never exhaust. As Christians we should constantly be uncovering new insights into his glory, seeing a little more fully the wonder of his grace and truth, for however much we may have glimpsed, there is always more to be revealed.

PENTECOST

35   People of the Spirit

Reading   Galatians 5:13-26

Aim   To highlight what should be essential characteristics of 'people of the Spirit'.

Preparation   Draw two large ovals and display these on separate whiteboards. Underneath one write CHRIS and under the other write IAN.

Next draw and cut out the following shapes (you will need to ensure they are to scale with other features of the face that you are going to create with them):

- Four ovals, to serve as eyes
- Two mouth shapes
- Four ear shapes
- Two irregular shapes, to serve as noses
- Two large crescent shapes to serve as hair
- Four smaller crescent shapes to serve as eyebrows

Try to make the two sets of features distinctive.

Print, in as large letters as possible, the following on the back of these shapes:

Ears	Self-control/Patience (one on each)
Nose	Kindness
Hair	Generosity
Eyes	Love/Peace (one on each)
Mouths	Gentleness
Eyebrows	Faithfulness/Joy (one on each)

Stick the shapes with a small piece of blutack in conspicuous places around the church, with the words facing downwards.

Talk   Tell the congregation that you need to draw up a photo-fit of a couple of people you've been hearing about called Chris and Ian. Ask people to look around the church and see if they can spot the parts of a face that you need to build up each picture. Ask in turn for a mouth, eye, nose, etc. until both faces are complete.

Tell people to have a good look at these and ask if anyone has seen them. Then announce that you've just realised that this is a case of mistaken identity, the character you're looking for being one person, or rather the name given to a certain kind of person and people. Ask if anyone can spot what the name is. The answer, of course, is Christian, the letter 'T' missing in between CHRIS and IAN.

So what does a Christian look like? To answer that we need only look around this or any other church. In other words, Christians come in all shapes and sizes, there being nothing physically different or distinctive about any of us. The difference is not on the outside, but the inside, so let's consider what we might find there. Turn over the various components of the faces, and read out what is on the back of each piece, either once again arranging these in the shape of a head, or simply displaying them at random. Love, joy, peace, patience, kindness, generosity, gentleness, faithfulness, self-control – these are the things that God wants to see in our lives, the sort of qualities that should characterise a Christian. The Bible calls them fruits of the Spirit, for these are not qualities we can acquire through our own efforts alone, coming rather through being open to God's Spirit and ready to let that Spirit work within us. Yet if God plays his part we must also play ours, looking to grow in faith, to respond to the Spirit's guidance and to cultivate our relationship with Christ. None of us recognised the photo-fit pictures we put together, because of course they weren't real people. The question is, will anyone recognise us as Christians, or will they see us too as a sham?

36   Experiencing the unseen

Readings   John 3:1-15; 1 Corinthians 12:1-12

Aim   To bring home the fact that though we cannot see the Holy Spirit, we can experience the Spirit's power in our lives and see evidence of it in the lives of other Christians.

Preparation   For this talk, all you need is a small portable radio, though make sure that the volume can be turned up loud enough for it to be heard throughout the church. You will need to have preset stations, or to know which frequencies various stations are tuned to.

Talk   Ask how many people listen to the radio, which station they like best, which programme they most like listening to, and who is their favourite DJ or presenter. Tell the congregation that you are going to give them a radio test. Tune one by one to the following stations, asking if people can guess which station each one is: Radio 2, Radio 4, local radio station, Classic FM, Radio 1, Radio 5, foreign radio station (as catch question), Radio 3, Virgin Radio, World Service. Take several answers, and perhaps a poll of the congregation each time, to ensure maximum participation among all those present.

All of those radio stations and programmes are being broadcast all over the country – in the case of the World Service, all over the world. The air is full of radio waves, not to mention TV signals, yet, of course, we cannot see any them, or hear them without a radio to receive them. We know they are there through experience, having simply to turn our radio on to prove it, but they themselves are hidden from human sight.

So it is also with the Holy Spirit. As Jesus told Nicodemus, when speaking of being born again, 'The wind blows where it chooses, and you hear the sound of it, but you do not know where it comes from or where it goes. So it is with everyone who is born of the Spirit' (John 3:8). We cannot pin down how the Holy Spirit works or through whom he works. We cannot physically prove to others that the Spirit is anything other than our imagination. But when we turn to Christ and commit ourselves to him, we experience the presence of the Spirit within us: the peace, power, guidance and inspiration that only the Spirit can give. And if the Spirit is indeed at work, then that will show in the way we live and the gifts we show, in whether the fruits of the Spirit are in evidence and our gifts used in his service.

As the Apostle Paul reminds us, '[w]e look not at what can be seen but at what cannot be seen; for what can be seen is temporary, but what cannot be seen is eternal (2 Corinthians 4:18). Though we cannot see the Spirit, never underestimate what he is able to do in our lives.

37   Fruit, not flowers

Readings   1 Corinthians 14:1-19; Galatians 5:16-26

Aim   To emphasise that the presence of the Holy Spirit is shown not by showy gifts but by living fruits.

Preparation   On separate strips of paper/card, print the following in large bold letters:

MARIGOLD, LUPINS, ANTIRRHINUM, GERANIUM, CHRYSANTHEMUM, ROSE, FUSCHIA, ASTER, DELPHINIUM, SWEET PEA, TOFFEE, MELBA, MERINGUE PIE, AND CREAM, AND CUSTARD, WINE, JUICE, SPLIT, FRITTERS, SORBET, ROLLS, PINEAPPLE, RHUBARB, LEMON, BANANA, PEACH, STRAWBERRIES, ORANGE, APPLE, MELON, FIG, ELDERBERRY

Attach magnetic tape or blutack to the back of each, and arrange on a board as follows:

MARIGOLD MERINGUE PIE

LUPINS AND CREAM

TOFFEE FUSCHIA

GERANIUM AND CUSTARD

ROSE MELBA

SWEET PEA WINE

ANTIRRHINUM JUICE

CHRYSANTHEMUM FRITTERS

ASTER SORBET

DELPHINIUM ROLLS

HOLLYHOCK SPLIT

Retain the remaining words for use later in the talk.

Talk   Ask the congregation how much they fancy the mouth-watering delicacies you have spelled out on the board. Express mock surprise at their disinterest, and ask what's wrong with the dishes – in other words, what they ought to read. As people come up with the answers, remove the wrong word and insert the correct one, as follows:

LEMON MERINGUE PIE

STRAWBERRIES AND CREAM

TOFFEE APPLE

RHUBARB AND CUSTARD

PEACH MELBA
ELDERBERRY WINE
ORANGE JUICE
PINEAPPLE FRITTERS
MELON SORBET
FIG ROLLS
BANANA SPLIT

There's nothing wrong, of course, with flowers – indeed, the world would be a sadder and less beautiful place without them – but we don't generally want to eat them. Fruit is a different matter. It *can* look attractive and even be grown for ornamental purposes, but we usually grow it for food, for the express purpose of eating. In some cases, flowers may be a stage on the way to fruit, but in terms of usefulness it's the fruit we're after.

Perhaps this is why Paul referred to various God-given qualities as 'fruits of the Spirit' – things like love, joy, peace, patience, kindness, generosity, faithfulness, gentleness and self-control. Not only can these qualities be seen but they also affect the way we live and the people we are. They are not simply there for show, but are a visible harvest of the Holy Spirit's presence within us.

So it is that Paul, writing to the Corinthians, warns of the danger of coveting showy spiritual gifts. Of course, gifts of the Spirit have their place, but only insofar as they are complemented by spiritual fruits, and, above all, by love. Pentecost reminds us of the day when power came upon the Apostles, enabling them to preach to a multitude in a variety of tongues, but we should never forget that it reminds us also of the way countless lives both then and across the centuries have been changed through the fruits of the Spirit being nurtured within them. How far do such fruits testify to the work of the Spirit within you?

TRINITY

38   Beyond comparison?

Readings Isaiah 40:18-26; 46:5-7; 2 Corinthians 13:13

Aim To emphasise the truth that the only way we can do justice to the wonder of God is through recognising him as Father, Son and Holy Spirit.

Preparation No special preparation is needed for this talk.

Talk Ask the congregation if they can define what a simile is (i.e. a word that compares one thing to another, using the word 'like' or 'as'). Ask if anyone can supply the missing word from each of the following well-known similes:

As common as ?	*muck*
As bald as a ?	*coot*
As tough as ?	*nails* (or *old boots*)
As meek as a ?	*lamb*
As bold as ?	*brass*
As ugly as ?	*sin*
As cool as a ?	*cucumber*
As fit as a ?	*flea* (or *fiddle*)
As daft as a ?	*brush*
As flat as a ?	*pancake*
As light as a ?	*feather*
As warm as ?	*toast*
As good as ?	*gold*
As mad as a ?	*hatter* (or *March hare*)
As pleased as ?	*Punch*
As pretty as ?	*a picture*
As clear as ?	*a bell* (or *as mud* or *as crystal*)
As red as a ?	*beetroot*
As safe as ?	*houses*
As snug as a ?	*bug in a rug*
As dull as ?	*ditchwater*
As straight as an ?	*arrow*
As keen as ?	*mustard*
As stubborn as a ?	*mule*
As white as a ?	*sheet*
As busy as a ?	*bee*
As clean as a ?	*whistle*

When it comes to God, comparisons are not just difficult but impossible, for every metaphor or simile we may use can, at best, point to a fraction of the truth, each concealing as much as it reveals. However many words we may pile up to speak of his power, love, grace or goodness, they will always be inadequate, for he is infinitely greater than all of them put together. As the prophet Isaiah puts it, 'To whom, then, will you liken God, or with what likeness will you compare him? An idol? It is cast by a workman and a goldsmith gilds it and casts silver chains for it. The one unable to afford this selects wood that will not rot and seeks out a craftsman to create an idol that will not topple over' (Isaiah 40:18-20, own translation). Or as the Psalmist asks, 'Who on high can compare to the Lord? Who among the heavenly host is like the Lord, a God revered in the assembly of the holy ones, great and awesome above all those around him?' (Psalm 89:5-7, own translation).

So does this mean that God is beyond comparison? Almost, but not quite, for though no words or image can hope to express his greatness, three terms give us some kind of picture of who he is: the terms 'Father', 'Son' and 'Holy Spirit'. The first reminds us that God is the giver of life but at the same time likens him to a father; one, in other words, who loves and cares for all his children. The second reminds us that God in Christ has shared our humanity, walking our earth and experiencing both life and death, and thus revealing God's nature and purpose through word and deed. The last reminds us that though we do not see him we experience God's presence within us, at work in our lives and in the world, nothing able to contain or limit him.

Trinity Sunday reminds us that we need to keep a sense of God's greatness that is beyond comparison, yet to recognise also the way we experience that God as Father, Son and Holy Spirit. So, along with the Apostle Paul, we can not only say with our lips but can also mean in our hearts: 'The grace of our Lord Jesus Christ, the love of God, and the companionship of the Holy Spirit, be with us all' (2 Corinthians 13:13, own translation).

39 A sense of proportion

Reading Ephesians 3:16-21

Aim To stress the importance of Trinity Sunday in reminding us of the overwhelming scale of God's greatness.

Preparation Print the following riddle on a large piece of card/paper, in large, bold letters.

My first is in MEGA as well as in GREAT,

My second's in WOW but not UNDERSTATE,

My third is in WONDER and found in ADORE.

My whole calls forth worship expressing our awe.

Print the riddle again in microscopic letters on a tiny piece of paper.

Talk Tell the congregation that you have a simple riddle for them to solve. Stick the tiny version on to a whiteboard, and ask who can solve it. Of course, no one will be able to because no one will be able to read it! Ask what the problem is, and then display the larger version. This time, the congregation should have no problem in solving the riddle to reveal the word GOD.

Often in life we need to get the bigger picture before we can understand what's going on, and the same is true when it comes to God. Our picture of him is often far too small, disproportionate to the reality. To illustrate what I mean, take a look at the following picture:

Ask what's wrong with the first picture, and allow people to identify all the features that are out of proportion. Afterwards, display the 'corrected' picture, as follows:

(Larger versions of these pictures may be found on pages 304-305 in the Photocopy Masters section.)

When drawing, we need to ensure that we keep things in their proper proportion, and the same is true when it comes to thinking about God, as we see in our reading today. Paul grasps at every proportion imaginable to express the wonder of God's love in Christ. 'I pray,' he writes, 'that Christ may so dwell in your hearts through faith that you will be able to grasp with all the saints the breadth, length, height and depth of the love of Christ; and that you may know this all-surpassing love in such a way that you will be filled with the very fullness of God!' (Ephesians 3:14a, 17-19, own translation). This love, says Paul, is beyond measure, bigger than anything we can ever begin to comprehend and reaching out in any and every direction, nothing and nowhere outside of its scope. And if that's true of God's love, it's all the more true when it comes to describing or defining God himself. However great we may believe he is, he is always greater still, on a scale that leaves us gasping in amazement. The only way we can begin to express that wonder is through the three labels, God the Father, God the Son and God the Holy Spirit. Why? Because those three persons point to his presence above, beside and within us, different dimensions of one reality. Overemphasise a single aspect at the cost of the others and our picture of God becomes distorted and unbalanced. We need a sense of God's majesty and splendour, an awareness of his constant companionship and friendship, and an experience of his power and presence deep within. All are part of the picture but none are the whole.

Don't let your picture of God be too small or out of proportion. Learn the message of Trinity and glimpse a little more clearly the breadth, length, height and depth of who God is and what he means.

ALL SAINTS' DAY

40   Keeping going

Readings

1 Corinthians 9:24-27; Hebrews 12:1-2

Aim

Through the example of those who have kept the faith, to point to the importance of perseverance in discipleship.

Preparation

For this talk you will need two wind-up or battery-powered novelty figures (available from gift boutiques, toy shops and so forth), the sort that waddle along on two legs. One of these needs to be fairly fast but tall and unstable, the other needs to be a little slower but short and squat, and thus more stable over uneven ground. For the purposes of description, I will refer to these as Figures A and B, but you may like to invent names for them, depending on the toys you choose. You will also need a long table or board for the toys to race on and a large thick cloth with which to cover the board/table for a later race.

Talk

Show the congregation your two toys and tell them that you are going to race them against each other. Take a show of hands as to who they think will win. Barring an unforeseen catastrophe, the taller and faster toy should win easily. Rerun the race a couple of times to show that this result was no fluke. Now spread the cloth over the table, rumpling it up to produce a slightly uneven surface, not sufficient to interrupt the progress of Figure B but enough to make Figure A topple over. Ask the congregation once more who they think will win, and then demonstrate. Again, rerun the race a couple of times to prove the result was no accident.

As long as the going is smooth, Figure A wins easily, but when it gets rough then Figure A comes unstuck and Figure B comes through to win, the only one able to complete the course. This calls to mind the words of a song from a film a few years back: 'When the going gets tough . . . the tough get going.' And that's exactly the message in our readings today, two passages that remind us the going isn't always easy when it comes to following Jesus. 'They were stoned to death,' says the book of Hebrews, 'they were sawn in two, they were killed by the sword; they went about in skins of sheep and goats, destitute, persecuted, tormented' (Hebrews 11:37). Thankfully, we today do not face such dangers for being Christians but it is still not always easy in a world where few have any time for the gospel, where life doesn't always go as we hope, and where we will encounter our fair share of difficulties and disappointments. It's easy to call ourselves Christians and to make an impulsive commitment, but will we be able to keep faith through thick and thin? If we are to do so we need to work at our faith and nurture our relationship with Christ. In the words of Paul, 'Do you not know that in a race the runners all compete, but only one receives the prize? Run in such a way that you may win it' (1 Corinthians 9:24). Or as the writer to the Hebrews puts it, 'Let us also lay aside every weight and the sin that clings so closely, and let us run with perseverance the race that is set before us, looking to Jesus the pioneer and perfecter of our faith' (Hebrews 12:1b-2a).

41   All saints together

Readings   1 Corinthians 1:1-3; Ephesians 2:11-22

Aim   To show that though we revere some especially as saints, in God's eyes we are all saints simply by being part of the Church.

Preparation   On separate strips of coloured card, print the following:

PARROTS, LIONS, GOLDFINCHES, BEES, KITTENS, BISHOPS, GEESE, PIPERS, ACROBATS, SHIPS, WOLVES, CROWS, FISH, DUCKS, LARKS, CATTLE, SHEEP

Affix magnetic tape or blutack to the back of each, and arrange on a board as shown below:

```
P A R R O T S
      L I O N S
            G O L D F I N C H E S
      B E E S
   K I T T E N S
   B I S H O P S
         G E E S E
   P I P E R S
A C R O B A T S
         S H I P S
   W O L V E S
            C R O W S
      F I S H
         D U C K S
      L A R K S
            C A T T L E
      S H E E P
```

On strips of card of a different colour, print the following:

GAGGLE, HERD, CHARM, SWARM, MURDER, PRIDE, SKIRL, LITTER, PADDLING, SHOAL, BENCH, PACK, PANDEMONIUM, ARMADA, FLOCK, TROUPE, EXALTATION

Affix magnetic tape or blutack to the back of each, and retain for use later in the talk, ideally for display on a second board.

Talk

Ask the congregation what we might call a collection or group of questions. Several answers could be given, such as 'an exam' or 'a test', but the one you are looking for is 'a quiz'. Explain that you have a quiz today concerned with the various groups of people, animals or objects listed on the board, some very easy, some very hard. Ask the following questions, and as each correct answer is given, display it on a second whiteboard, as shown after the quiz questions:

1. What do we call a group of wolves? A *PACK*
2. What do we call a group of pipers? A *SKIRL*
3. What do we call a group of ducks? A *PADDLING*
4. What do we call a group of fish? A *SHOAL*
5. What do we call a group of ships? AN *ARMARDA*
6. What do we call a group of lions? A *PRIDE*
7. What do we call a group of parrots? *A PANDEMONIUM*
8. What do we call a group of larks? AN *EXALTATION*
9. What do we call a group of bees? A *SWARM*
10. What do we call a group of kittens? A *LITTER*
11. What do we call a group of sheep? A *FLOCK*
12. What do we call a group of geese? A *GAGGLE*
13. What do we call a group of crows? A *MURDER*
14. What do we call a group of acrobats? A *TROUPE*
15. What do we call a group of cattle? A *HERD*
16. What do we call a group of bishops? A *BENCH*
17. What do we call a group of goldfinches? A *CHARM*

```
          P A C K
    S K I R L
    P A D D L I N G
            S H O A L
      A R M A D A
          P R I D E
          P A N D E M O N I U M
    E X A L T A T I O N
            S W A R M
        L I T T E R
        F L O C K
            G A G G L E
    M U R D E R
              T R O U P E
          H E R D
        B E N C H
      C H A R M
```

Without commenting yet on the arrangement of questions and answers, ask what we call a collection of Christians. The answer you are looking for is 'a church'. Ask what we call a collection of churches. The answer you are looking for this time is '*the* Church'. There is, however, another answer we could give to both those questions. Ask if anyone can think what word we might use to cover both a collection of Christians and a collection of churches. The answer is 'saints'. We tend to use the term for a select few, those who have shown special faith or holiness in their lives, but in the original Greek of the New Testament it is applied to all those who love and follow Jesus. So Paul starts the first of his letters to the Corinthians (1:2): 'To the church of God that is in Corinth, to those who are sanctified in Christ, called to be saints, together with all those who in every place call on the name of our Lord Jesus Christ, both their Lord and ours.' Or as he wrote similarly to the Ephesians (2:19): 'You are, therefore, no longer strangers and aliens, but fellow-citizens with the saints and members of God's family.' Those words apply not just to then but to now, not simply to those Paul was writing to in Corinth and Ephesus, but to all who have committed their lives to Christ. We are part of the family of God's people in every age, and those who will share in the inheritance of his eternal kingdom. The answer is there in the questions and answers of our quiz. Ask if anyone can see the two hidden messages – TOGETHER THE CHURCH and ALL SAINTS TOGETHER. In other words, we are all different, just like the various groups we've looked at – each reflecting a unique blend of background, temperament and circumstances that has made us what we are – but as Christians, we are not only TOGETHER THE CHURCH but also, by God's grace, ALL SAINTS TOGETHER.

NEW YEAR

42   A new chapter

Reading

Psalm 116

Aim

To recall God's faithfulness across the years, and so to look forward to the future in hope and confidence.

Preparation

No special preparation is needed for this talk.

Talk

Tell the congregation that you want to think about stories, specifically about autobiographies written by celebrities past and present. Ask who wrote the following (you may wish to add other more recent titles or personal favourites to the list):

Single Minded	Cliff Richard
Taken on Trust	Terry Waite
Opening Up	Mike Atherton
Steve Redgrave: A Golden Age	Steve Redgrave
Behind the White Ball	Jimmy White
Serious	John McEnroe
Crying with Laughter	Bob Monkhouse
No Half Measures	Graeme Souness
Quite Contrary	Mary Whitehouse
Heading for Victory	Steve Bruce
All Creatures Great and Small	James Herriot
The Downing Street Years	Margaret Thatcher
My Tune	Simon Bates
True	Martin Kemp
News From The Front	Sandy Gall
Walking on Water	Brian Clough
Managing My Life	Sir Alex Ferguson
Unless I'm very much mistaken	Murray Walker
Robbie Williams: Somebody, Someday	Robbie Williams
Saved	Tony Bullimore
Nothing Like a Dame	Thora Hird
Learning to Fly	Victoria Beckham
Trowel and Error	Alan Titchmarsh
Gareth Gates: Right from the Start	Gareth Gates

All of these are written by famous people and consequently of huge interest to many. Our own stories may not quite capture the public imagination in the same way, but we all have a story to tell – our own unique experiences, our own journey through life – and as Christians that includes a story of faith: the way God called us to respond to his love in Christ; the way he has led us over the years; the way he has nurtured, strengthened, comforted and inspired, leading us to where we are today.

As we stand on the threshold of another year, this is an opportunity to reflect on such things, and, in remembering God's faithfulness, to look forward to another chapter in our own continuing story. We do not know how the plot will unravel in the days ahead, what new pages might be written, but we do know that we can trust the author of life itself and the one who has written our names in the pages of the book of life.

43   Looking to the future

Readings

Jeremiah 29:10-14; Revelation 21:1-4

Aim

To emphasise that God holds the future in his hands, and that, whatever that future may hold, we can trust him in all things to work for good, sure of his eternal purpose.

Preparation

No special preparation is needed for this talk.

Talk

Ask the congregation what name we give to novels, films or TV programmes set in the future, either depicting what life on earth might become one day or set in far-flung galaxies of the universe. The answer, of course, is science fiction. Tell the congregation that you have prepared a quiz for them with a science-fiction flavour:

- Which long-running television programme followed the fortunes of a Time Lord? *Dr Who*
- Which film had as its chief villain the Emperor Ming? *Flash*
- Which film featured dinosaurs recreated from ancient DNA? *Jurassic Park* (1 and 2)
- Which old TV space series featured a computer called Orac? *Blake's 7*
- Which hugely popular space film spawned two sequels and (to date) two prequels? *Star Wars*
- Which book by George Orwell was about a year in the future that is now long past? *1984*
- Which Stephen Spielberg science-fiction film featured a lovable extra-terrestrial? *ET*
- Which Stephen Spielberg film focuses on meetings with aliens? *Close Encounters of the Third Kind*
- Which book by Aldous Huxley warned of dehumanisation in a scientific age? *Brave New World*
- Which humorous space series by Douglas Adams was first broadcast on the radio? *A Hitch Hiker's Guide to the Galaxy*
- Which series featured Captain Kirk of the Starship Enterprise? *Star Trek*
- Which classic science-fiction book was about giant plants? *The Day of the Triffids*
- What space film is set at the beginning of this millennium? *2001: A Space Odyssey*
- Which classic book is about interplanetary warfare? *The War of the Worlds*

- Which author created the hugely successful *Discworld* series of books? *Terry Pratchett*
- Which Old Testament prophet looked forward to the world of the future? *Jeremiah*
- Which book of the New Testament focuses on last times and God's kingdom? *Revelation*

Each of the above painted a picture of what the world might be like in the future, but all except two represent mere speculation – all, that is, except for Jeremiah and the book of Revelation. Whereas the other authors wrote about what *might* happen, Jeremiah and Revelation speak of what *will* happen. In Jeremiah's case, he spoke first to the people of Israel concerning an end to their time in Israel, but his words generally concerning God's plans apply to us and all those who trust in God's purpose. 'For surely I know the plans I have for you, says the Lord, plans for your welfare and not for harm, to give you a future with hope' (Jeremiah 29:11). This, of course, is not to say that we are guaranteed immunity from life's troubles, that everything will work out just as we want, that we are guaranteed good things, but it *is* to say that ultimately God holds our future in his hands, and that nothing can separate us from his love and eternal blessing. Whatever the future may bring, we can look forward to his kingdom, an unforgettable picture of which is painted in the book of Revelation. We do not know every detail of the future, either in this life or the life to come, but we know that God will be with us every step of the way, and that his promise will not fail. In that assurance, let us welcome this new year with hope, confidence, trust and thanksgiving.

44   New beginnings

Reading   2 Corinthians 5:16-21

Aim   To bring home the fact that with God not just every year but every day and moment is a new beginning.

Preparation   Print the following words in large bold letters, and stick them in prominent positions around the church:

LIGHT
PIN
LEAF
WOMAN/MAN
MOON
TRICKS
BROOM
BLOOD
JERSEY
LOOK
ENGLAND
WORLD
BORN
YEAR

Talk   Ask the congregation if they can think of one word that can be applied to all of the words on display. The word you are looking for is NEW. Now ask people to look around at the walls, and to see if they can find the words that match the clues you are going to give them.

1. We talk of seeing something in a new [what?] – *New light*
2. We sometimes use the expression 'as bright as a new [what?]' – *New pin*
3. When we resolve to change, we speak of 'turning over a new [what?]' – *New leaf*
4. When we've recovered from an illness we might talk of 'feeling like a new [what?] or [what?]'? *New woman or new man*
5. A lunar phase – *New moon*
6. We sometimes say that 'you can't teach an old dog new [what]'? *New tricks*
7. A new [what?] sweeps clean – *New broom*
8. We sometimes say this is needed if ideas have grown stale – *New blood*
9. This sounds like an addition to our wardrobe but the answer is in fact an American state – *New Jersey*

10. This sounds like you're viewing something but in fact it is a clothes store – *New Look*

11. This sounds close to home but is in fact in America – *New England*

12. This new [what?] sounds like it may harbour extra-terrestrial life but is in fact the name once given to a continent very much on this planet – *New World*

13. This is the term used for recently arrived offspring – *Newborn*

14. This is often seen as the time for resolutions – *New Year*

All of these in some way are, or at least were, about new beginnings, making a fresh start, and of course there is a very strong sense of that in the last example: New Year. This is a time, as indicated in the clue, when many make resolutions, but even if you don't do that there is always, if only briefly, a sense of starting again as we say goodbye to one year and hello to another. Sadly, it doesn't usually last for long, old habits dying hard and both the world and ourselves proving to be much the same despite the passing of another twelve months. Yet at the heart of our faith is the promise that things can be different, that we really can start again, not just at the beginning of the year but at any time, any moment of our lives. As Paul puts it in his second letter to the Corinthians (5:17): 'If anyone is in Christ, there is a new creation: everything old has passed away; see, everything has become new!' It may not always feel like that, for, though ultimately defeated, the old self lives on, repeatedly rearing its ugly head, but God is always ready to wipe the slate clean and give us another opportunity. That is the conviction in which we enter this new year: that ours is a God able to make us new; a God who, however often we fail, will be ready to pick us up, forgive us, and help us to start again.

WEEK OF PRAYER FOR CHRISTIAN UNITY

45   Working together

Reading   1 Corinthians 12:4-6, 12-13

Aim   Using the analogy of an orchestra, to bring home the fact that Christians of all denominations have a vital part to play in God's purpose, working in harmony together.

Preparation   Print in large letters on pieces of card the following words, one for each instrument:

> FLUTE, HARP, TROMBONE, DRUM, TRIANGLE, HORN, TUBA, HARPSICHORD, CELLO, BASSOON, DOUBLE BASS, VIOLA, CLARINET, OBOE, TRUMPET, PIANO, VIOLIN, CYMBALS

Attach a piece of magnetic tape to the back of each.

Talk   Tell the congregation you have prepared a quiz for them. From the clues you are about to give, they have to guess which orchestral instruments you are referring to. As each answer is given, set out the answers exactly as they are displayed on the next page. Take care to align them precisely.

1. A woodwind instrument which you hold sideways – *FLUTE*
2. A stringed instrument which is plucked – *HARP*
3. A brass instrument often used in jazz – *TROMBONE*
4. An instrument which is hit with sticks – *DRUM*
5. Sounds like a geometrical shape – *TRIANGLE*
6. Sounds like part of a car – *HORN*
7. A large and heavy brass instrument – *TUBA*
8. A keyboard instrument that is plucked – *HARPSICHORD*
9. A stringed instrument rhyming with hello – *CELLO*
10. The largest and deepest woodwind instrument – *BASSOON*
11. The largest and deepest stringed instrument – *DOUBLE BASS*
12. Sounds like a flower – *VIOLA*
13. A woodwind instrument often used in jazz – *CLARINET*
14. A woodwind instrument which has a double reed – *OBOE*
15. An instrument which you might find in a brass band – *TRUMPET*
16. A keyboard instrument, the Latin word for which means 'soft' – *PIANO*
17. The instrument played by Nigel Kennedy – *VIOLIN*
18. Flat dishes which clang together – *CYMBALS*

```
              F L U T E
                  H A R P
      T R O M B O N E
              D R U M
      T R I A N G L E
                  H O R N


                  T U B A
    H A R P S I C H O R D
                  C E L L O
          B A S S O O N
      D O U B L E   B A S S


          V I O L A
          C L A R I N E T
          O B O E


          T R U M P E T
          P I A N O
      V I O L I N
              C Y M B A L S
```

Ask if anyone in the congregation can spot the hidden message –
THOUGH THESE ARE MANY. Now, tell the congregation you
are going to rearrange the words to finish off the hidden message.
Rearrange as follows, again taking care to align the words precisely:

```
              T R O M B O N E
    B A S S O O N
    T R I A N G L E
        F L U T E
C L A R I N E T
              H O R N
      O B O E
      D R U M

              T U B A
H A R P S I C H O R D
          C E L L O
          C Y M B A L S

      P I A N O
      H A R P
  D O U B L E   B A S S

      V I O L A
  V I O L I N
  T R U M P E T
```

Ask if anybody can see the second part of the message – TOGETHER
THEY ARE ONE.

THOUGH THESE ARE MANY, TOGETHER THEY ARE
ONE. And of course that is exactly right, for put these instruments
together and they form a single orchestra. What of the Church?
How far do these words apply there? As individual Christians we
are certainly many, each of us different, with our own ideas and own
experiences of God, but through Christ we have been joined together
to form one people, one fellowship.

But it doesn't end there, for there are many other Christians outside our own fellowship, both within our particular denomination
and beyond. The fact is that Christians have different ways of doing
things, different ways of worshipping, different types of service, and
sometimes even different interpretations of various aspects of faith. But
though we are many, we are still nonetheless one, all serving the same
God, all part of the same family, all working for the same kingdom.

We may have different roles and different contributions to make,
but it is only when we work together that God's purpose can finally
be complete.

46   Bound together

Readings   Ephesians 4:15-16; 1 Corinthians 12:1-13, 27-31

Aim   To recognise our differences as Christians, but also to emphasise the unity that should characterise the Church.

Preparation   For this talk, you will need the following (empty containers/packets will do for many): wallpaper paste, glue stick, blutack, bonding adhesive, Copydex, wood glue, UHU glue, sticky tape, parcel tape, superglue, a small quantity of cement.

Talk   Tell the congregation that you have a talk this week that will have them glued to their seats! Display the various items you have collected together and ask what they have in common. The answer, of course, is that they all stick things together – only it's not quite that simple. Ask which of us, for example, would try to stick paper with cement, or to cement bricks with wallpaper paste, or to hang wallpaper with blutack? None of us would even consider it. Different jobs require different glues if they're to be done properly; there is a right one for each. Go through each item, and ask what sort of sticking job people might use it for.

There's a simple lesson in all this for the Church, because like these various adhesives we are all different. That's what Paul was saying in his letter to the Corinthians: we are not the same, each of us being designed by God for a particular role, a certain function. Yet we are all nonetheless one. Just as the items we looked at were all adhesives, *we* are all Christians.

And that leads to a second point, and the reason why this talk is about glue, sticky tape and so on, for just as these fasten things together so we should be bound together by the love of Christ. As Paul wrote to the Ephesians (4:15-16, own translation):

> Lovingly speaking the truth, we must in every aspect grow up into the head; that is, into Christ; through whom each part of the body – joined and knitted together by its supporting ligaments so that each may function as it should – grows and builds itself up in love.

There is no need for different kinds of adhesives here: the glue that binds us together, irrespective of our differences, is the love of Christ. So then, in this week of prayer for Christian Unity, let us respect our diversity yet remember our unity, recognising that what-ever may divide us we are all united in the same Lord, the same faith, the same love.

47   Though we are many

Reading   1 Corinthians 12:4-6, 12-13

Aim   To bring home the fact that truth can be expressed in many different ways, a fact reflected in the diversity of the Church.

Preparation   For this talk you will either need various translations of the Bible, each open or marked at the appropriate place, or, perhaps better, you can print translations of the verses below. In either case, do not reveal when reading the passages which translation you are reading from.

New Revised Standard Version
Now there are varieties of gifts, but the same Spirit; and there are varieties of services, but the same Lord; and there are varieties of activities, but it is the same God who activates all of them in everyone. For just as the body is one and has many members, and all the members of the body, though many, are one body, so it is with Christ. For in the one Spirit, we were all baptised into one body – Jews or Greeks, slaves or free – and we were all made to drink of one Spirit.

Authorised Version (King James)
Now there are diversities of gifts, but the same Spirit. And there are differences of administrations, but the same Lord. And there are diversities of operations, but it is the same God which worketh all in all. For as the body is one, and hath many members, and all the members of that one body, being many, are one body: so also is Christ. For by one Spirit we are all baptised into one body, whether we be Jews or Gentiles, whether we be bond or free: and have been all made to drink into one Spirit.

New International Version
There are different kinds of gifts, but the same Spirit. There are different kinds of service, but the same Lord. There are different kinds of working, but the same God works all of them in all men. The body is a unit, though it is made up of many parts; and though all its parts are many, they form one body. So it is with Christ. For we were all baptised by one Spirit into one body – whether Jews or Greeks, slave or free – and we were all given the one Spirit to drink.

New English Bible
There are varieties of gifts, but the same Spirit. There are varieties of service, but the same Lord. There are many forms of work, but all of

them, in all men, are the work of the same God. For Christ is like a single body with its many limbs and organs, which, many as they are, together make up one body. For indeed we were all brought into one body by baptism, in the one Spirit, whether we are Jews or Greeks, whether slaves or free men, and that one Holy Spirit was poured out for all of us to drink.

Jerusalem Bible
There is a variety of gifts but always the same Spirit; there are all sorts of service to be done, but always to the same Lord; working in all sorts of different ways in different people, it is the same God who is working in all of them. Just as a human body, though it is made up of many parts, is a single unit because all these parts, though many, make one body, so it is with Christ. In the one Spirit we were all baptised, Jews as well as Greeks, slaves as well as citizens, and one Spirit was given to us all to drink.

You also need to print the following on separate strips of paper, and display them on a whiteboard, using blutack or magnetic tape so that you can rearrange them as necessary.

New Revised Standard Version (NRSV)

Authorised Version (or AV, or King James Bible)

New International Version (NIV)

New English Bible (NEB)

Jerusalem Bible

(You may wish to add your own versions and corresponding translations of the verse in question, to complement the list above.)

Talk   Tell the congregation that you are going to read them some verses from the Bible, and that you want them to identify which translation they are taken from. Display the list of alternatives you prepared earlier, and then, reading the various translations in turn, take a show of hands each time concerning the translation you are using. Rearrange the list of translations, in the order the congregation decides on. Afterwards, run through the readings again, giving the correct translation (and reordering your display) as necessary.

Ask which was the correct version. Of course, none of them is either correct or incorrect, each being a translation, and therefore interpretation, of the original Greek text, which itself is an attempt to interpret a God-given insight through words. The fact is that there are many ways of expressing the same truth, all of which are equally valid.

That's a lesson we need to keep constantly in mind when it comes to thinking about the Church. Despite the efforts that have been made over the years to break down barriers between Christians, the

Church is still fragmented into different groups: Anglicans, Catholics, Evangelicals, Liberals, High Church, Low Church, Traditionalists, Charismatics, to name but a few. So which are right and which are wrong? Which have the truth and which are misguided? The answer once again, of course, is all and none of them. Each expresses in different ways the truth of the gospel, bringing different experiences, histories, insights and characteristics to bear on their interpretation. None has the whole truth but all strive after it. Just as there are many translations but one Bible, so there are many denominations but one Church. Together, we give expression to the love of God made known and experienced through Jesus Christ our Lord.

MOTHERING
SUNDAY

48   Loving hands

Readings   Psalm 31:9-24; Isaiah 42:5-9

Aim   To bring home the fact that God holds each one of us in his hands, and to explore the implications of what that means. (The talk is well complemented by the hymn 'I trust in thee, O Lord'.)

Preparation   For this talk you will need to either copy, and perhaps enlarge, the pictures shown under Talk, below, or prepare similar illustrations of your own. (Larger versions of the pictures given here may be found in the Photocopy Masters section on pages 306-311.)

You will also need to write or print the following Bible verses (from a variety of translations) in large bold letters on to the largest sheets of paper you can find, sticking these up in prominent positions around the church.

As a mother comforts her child, so will I comfort you.
(Isaiah 66:13a)

Our steps are made firm by the Lord, when he delights in our way; though we stumble, we shall not fall headlong, for the Lord holds us by the hand. (Psalm 37:23-24)

I am always with you; you hold me by my right hand. You guide me with your counsel. (Psalm 73:23-24a)

I am the Lord your God, who takes hold of your right hand and says to you, 'Do not fear, I will help you.' (Isaiah 41:13)

Be strong and courageous. Do not be afraid, do not be discouraged, for the Lord your God will be with you wherever you go.
(Joshua 1:9)

See, the Sovereign Lord comes with power . . . He tends his flock like a shepherd; he gathers the lambs in his arms and carries them close to his heart. (Isaiah 40:10a, 11)

My child, do not despise the Lord's discipline, and do not resent his rebuke, because the Lord disciplines those he loves.
(Proverbs 3:11-12)

Every good and perfect gift is from above, coming down from the Father. (James 1:17)

He makes grass grow for the cattle, and plants for man to cultivate – bringing forth food from the earth, bread that sustains the heart. All look to you to give them their food at the proper time. When you give it to them, they gather it up; when you open your hand, they are satisfied with good things. (Psalm 104:14-15, 28)

Why worry about clothes? Look how the wild flowers grow: they do not work or make clothes for themselves. But I tell you that not even Solomon with all his wealth had clothes as beautiful as these flowers. It is God who clothes the wild grass . . . Won't he be all the more sure to clothe you? (Matthew 6:28-30)

Now then, my children, listen to me. Listen to my instruction and be wise, do not ignore it. (Proverbs 8:32)

I will look after those that are lost, bring back those that wander off, bandage those who are hurt, and heal those that are sick. (Ezekiel 34:16)

Talk   Tell the congregation that you want to think today about hands, and what these say to us about mothers and about God. Ask first whether anyone can identify commonly used expressions, all containing the word 'hard' from the following clues:

- Under control – *In hand*
- Being there when needed – *On hand*
- Applies discipline when necessary – *A firm hand*
- Involved in the action, not at a distance – *Hands on*
- Something given free – *Handout*
- Specially and personally chosen – *Hand-picked*
- Given carte blanche; complete discretion – *A free hand*
- Assured of safe keeping, being well looked after – *In good hands*
- Associated with Christian healing – *The laying on of hands*
- Sharing the load, offering help – *Lending a hand*
- A sign of welcome – *Handshake*
- Identifying with a person or people – *Throwing in one's hand with someone*
- Describes something we have made – *Handiwork* (or *handicraft*)

These are all expressions that we can apply in different ways to mothers. To illustrate this look at the following pictures of a mother and child, and see if you can guess what the mother is doing in each case.

Comforting

Supporting

Guiding

Keeping safe/protecting

Reassuring

Embracing/holding

Disciplining/telling off

Giving

Providing

Clothing

Teaching

Tending

These are just some of the many ways in which mothers care for and look after us, sometimes not only during childhood but beyond. But if they apply to mothers, they apply also to God, as the various verses displayed around the church show. (Run through the pictures again, asking if anyone can find a verse to match each one.)

Comforting
As a mother comforts her child, so will I comfort you.
(Isaiah 66:13a)

Supporting
Our steps are made firm by the Lord, when he delights in our way; though we stumble, we shall not fall headlong, for the Lord holds us by the hand. (Psalm 37:23-24)

Guiding
I am always with you; you hold me by my right hand. You guide me with your counsel. (Psalm 73:23-24a)

Keeping safe/protecting
I am the Lord your God, who takes hold of your right hand and says to you, 'Do not fear, I will help you.' (Isaiah 41:13)

Reassuring
Be strong and courageous. Do not be afraid, do not be discouraged, for the Lord your God will be with you wherever you go.
(Joshua 1:9)

Embracing/holding
See, the Sovereign Lord comes with power . . . He tends his flock like a shepherd; he gathers the lambs in his arms and carries them close to his heart. (Isaiah 40:10a, 11)

Disciplining/telling off
My child, do not despise the Lord's discipline, and do not resent his rebuke, because the Lord disciplines those he loves.
(Proverbs 3:11-12)

Giving
Every good and perfect gift is from above, coming down from the Father. (James 1:17)

Providing
He makes grass grow for the cattle, and plants for man to cultivate – bringing forth food from the earth, bread that sustains the heart. All look to you to give them their food at the proper time. When

you give it to them, they gather it up; when you open your hand, they are satisfied with good things. (Psalm 104:14-15, 28)

Clothing

Why worry about clothes? Look how the wild flowers grow: they do not work or make clothes for themselves. But I tell you that not even Solomon with all his wealth had clothes as beautiful as these flowers. It is God who clothes the wild grass . . . Won't he be all the more sure to clothe you? (Matthew 6:28-30)

Teaching

Now then, my children, listen to me. Listen to my instruction and be wise, do not ignore it. (Proverbs 8:32)

Tending

I will look after those that are lost, bring back those that wander off, bandage those who are hurt, and heal those that are sick. (Ezekiel 34:16)

In other words, mothers aren't alone in caring for us in these ways; God does too. Today is a day for remembering mothers – for sending cards, giving flowers or simply expressing how much they mean or meant to us – but it is also a day for remembering how much God loves us and values us as his children. So we can gladly join with David in saying, 'I trust in you, O Lord; I acknowledge that you are my God; my times are in your hands' (Psalm 31:14, own translation).

49   Learning from mothers

Readings   Various Bible verses are integral to this talk (see under Preparation and Talk).

Aim   To consider what a mother's love can teach us about the love God has for us.

Preparation   On large sheets of paper, print the following in bold, clearly visible letters and display in different positions around the church. Allow sufficient space for the missing word to be inserted later in the talk.

As a mother comforts her child, so I will _____ you. (Isaiah 66:13)

The Lord is good, his steadfast _____ endures for ever. (Psalm 100:5)

My child, do not despise the Lord's _____. (Proverbs 3:11)

God is our refuge and strength, a very present _____ in trouble. (Psalm 46:1)

God himself will _____ the lamb. (Genesis 22:8a)

_____ the weak hands, and make firm the feeble knees. (Isaiah 35:3)

I will _____ over them to build and to plant, says the Lord. (Jeremiah 31:28b)

Come, let us return to the Lord . . . and he will _____ us. (Hosea 6:1)

_____ me, O God, for in you I take refuge. (Psalm 16:1)

Cast all your anxiety on him, because he _____ for you. (1 Peter 5:7)

He will come and _____ you. (Isaiah 35:4b)

The Lord will _____ you continually. (Isaiah 58:11a)

If we confess our sins, he who is faithful and just will _____ us. (1 John 1:9a)

He will _____ his flock like a shepherd. (Isaiah 40:11a)

I will instruct you and _____ you the way you should go. (Psalm 32:8a)

Give ear, O Lord, to my prayer; _____ to my cry of supplication. (Psalm 86:6)

If God so clothes the grass of the field . . . how much more will he _____ you. (Luke 12:28)

On separate pieces of card, print the letters comprising the word-search on the following page, using the same size lettering as in the Bible verses above, and arrange on a whiteboard as shown, using blutack to stick the letters to the board.

N	E	H	T	G	N	E	R	T	S
P	L	O	V	E	H	C	T	A	W
R	E	L	I	S	T	E	N	F	E
O	H	F	S	E	R	A	C	O	D
T	T	E	H	E	L	P	H	R	I
E	O	E	E	V	A	S	H	G	V
C	L	D	H	E	A	L	A	I	O
T	C	G	U	I	D	E	E	V	R
T	R	O	F	M	O	C	T	E	P
D	I	S	C	I	P	L	I	N	E

Talk   Ask what are the first two words of the Lord's Prayer. The answer, of course, is 'Our Father', and that is the way we tend to think of God: as a father. Announce that because today is Mothering Sunday you want instead to consider God in terms of motherhood, asking what we might learn from mothers about who and what God is like.

Explain that you have prepared a word-search to help you do that. It contains 17 words that describe the sort of things mothers do or feel for us. Ask if people can find them and then find a verse somewhere in the church in which the word they have found fits. When they have done so, remove the appropriate letters from the board and reassemble them to fill in the missing word in the Bible verse. The complete verses are as follows:

As a mother comforts her child, so I will COMFORT you. (Isaiah 66:13)

The Lord is good; his steadfast LOVE endures for ever. (Psalm 100:5)

My child, do not despise the Lord's DISCIPLINE. (Proverbs 3:11)

God is our refuge and strength, a very present HELP in trouble. (Psalm 46:1)

God himself will PROVIDE the lamb. (Genesis 22:8a)

STRENGTHEN the weak hands, and make firm the feeble knees. (Isaiah 35:3)

I will WATCH over them to build and to plant, says the Lord. (Jeremiah 31:28b)

Come, let us return to the Lord . . . and he will HEAL us. (Hosea 6:1a)

PROTECT me, O God, for in you I take refuge. (Psalm 16:1)

Cast all your anxiety on him, because he CARES for you.
(1 Peter 5:7)

He will come and SAVE you. (Isaiah 35:4b)

The Lord will GUIDE you continually. (Isaiah 58:11a)

If we confess our sins, he who is faithful and just will FORGIVE us. (1 John 1:9a)

He will FEED his flock like a shepherd. (Isaiah 40:11a)

I will instruct you and TEACH you the way you should go.
(Psalm 32:8a)

Give ear, O Lord, to my prayer; LISTEN to my cry of supplication.
(Psalm 86:6)

If God so clothes the grass of the field . . . how much more will he CLOTHE you. (Luke 12:28)

We celebrate Mothering Sunday for two reasons. First, it reminds us of how much mothers do for us – the sort of things we have thought of today. Second, the example set by mothers reminds us how God loves and cares for us in turn, watching over us and caring for us in a multitude of ways. Give thanks for mothers, give thanks to God, and celebrate all that they mean and do within our lives.

CHRISTIAN AID WEEK

50   Neighbours

Reading   Luke 10:25-37

Aim   To bring home the fact that, in God's eyes, anyone in need is potentially our neighbour.

Preparation   No special preparation is needed for this talk.

Talk   Ask where would you find the following living as neighbours? (Given that soap-opera characters are constantly changing, you may need to substitute different names to those given in the lists below.)

- *Ramsay Street*
  Harold Bishop
  Susan Kennedy
  Lou Carpenter
  Lyn Scully
- *Albert Square*
  Pat Evans
  Phil Mitchell
  Ian Beale
  Pauline Fowler
- *Coronation Street*
  Ken Barlow
  Vera Duckworth
  Mike Baldwin
  Audrey Roberts
- *Emmerdale*
  Edna Birch
  Marlon Dingle
  Alan Turner
  Diane Blackstock
- *Downing Street*
  Prime Minister
  Chancellor of the Exchequer
- *Give the name of the road/street in which your church is situated*
  Give the names of four people living in the same road/street as your church

All of these – even though most are fictitious – are neighbours in the traditional sense of living next door to/or in the same street/vicinity as each other. But the word 'neighbour' or 'neighbouring' can be understood in a much broader sense. Can anyone, for example, think of the county, country and continent respectively that is neighbour to the following:

- *Gloucestershire, Wiltshire, Berkshire, Buckinghamshire, Northamptonshire and Warwickshire*
  Oxfordshire

- *France, Germany, The Netherlands*
  Belgium

- *North America*
  South America

Neighbours are not necessarily those living next door. It's a common-place to observe that we live in a small world, but today, in our inter-net and satellite age, that's more true than ever. So who is our neighbour in a context such as this? According to Jesus, the answer is simple: it is anyone we come across in need. Whether it is some-body down our street or living in some distant continent, through responding to their need we honour the commandment to love our neighbour as ourselves.

That, essentially, is what Christian Aid reminds us of. It highlights the plight of the poor in so many parts of our world: people we will never meet, countries we will probably never visit, and situations we may quite possibly never fully understand, yet those within them are our neighbours in need of our help. We cannot respond to all, but we cannot and should not ignore them either. As Jesus himself reminds us, when we respond to even one person, we respond also to him. We are challenged today to recognise our common humanity, and to respond as neighbours.

51 A raw deal

Reading Matthew 25:1-46

Aim To illustrate the inequalities of this world and the unfairness under-lying them, and to ask in what way we intend to respond to these.

Preparation You will need two packs of playing cards. Prepare one pack so that when you deal two hands of thirteen cards each, starting from the top, the first hand ends up with four 2's, four 3's, four 4's, and a 5, while the second hands ends up with four Aces, four Kings, four Queens, and one Jack in the same suit as the five in hand one. From the second pack, prepare two more hands (for display purposes only), the first having three Aces, three Kings, three Queens, and a Jack (use hearts, diamonds and clubs only) and the second having a complete set of spades, two up to Ace.

Talk Tell the congregation you fancy playing a game of cards and ask if anyone is willing to play a hand with you? Select a volunteer (making sure they are old enough to understand the basic rules of whist) and then deal out two hands from the first pack you rigged earlier. Give the first hand to the volunteer and keep the second for yourself. Explain that you will be playing by the rules of whist (i.e. Aces high, trumping allowed only when unable to follow suit). Announce to the congregation that you are going to choose trumps (the suit that you have four cards of) and then tell them that, to make things more interesting for them, you are going to show them the two hands first! Display both hands of cards and ask whether the congregation thinks the game will be a fair contest. Light-heartedly brush off their protests, and proceed to play. You will, of course, win every trick!

Express sympathy with your opponent and thank them for their help. Display the other two sets of hands that you prepared before the service, and ask the congregation if this would give a fairer game. The answer this time depends on who chooses trumps. If your opponent chooses, he or she will win every trick; if you choose, then you will win them all.

What has all this to do with Christian Aid, you may ask – and if you put this question to the congregation, you may very well get some intelligent answers offering a useful lead-in to the rest of the talk! The answer is that, in terms of the world as a whole, we are those who have been dealt a good hand; those who hold all the cards when it comes to securing the spoils. We may not be rich compared to many in this country, but compared to the majority in what we call the Third World, we are those who have been dealt all the cards, who are incomparably wealthy. Do we recognise how fortunate we are? Do we remember those less fortunate? Do we give from our plenty so that all may have some share in this earth's bounty?

There's a second and more disturbing point to be made, arising from the second set of hands we looked at, for what we saw there was that who wins depends on who has first choice; on who, in other words, holds the power in the contest. In terms of world affairs and economic systems, the answer to that is very clear: for centuries it has been the Western world that has called the tune, and those whom we label the Third World have been engaged in a game of catch-up that they haven't the slightest hope of winning. Power rests firmly in the hands of prosperous nations and their governments, and, more recently, in the hands of giant corporations and multi-nationals; the pack is loaded against so-called developing countries.

We all know, if we are honest, that we are part of an unjust world, a divided world of rich and poor. Well fed and hungry, haves and have-nots. What are we going to do about it? What response are we, personally, going to make?

52   Actions speak louder than words

Readings   Matthew 25:31-46; James 1:22-27; 2:14-17

Aim   To emphasise the importance of showing our faith in action.

Preparation   No special preparation is needed for this talk, but you may want to practise making the gestures indicated under 'Talk', perhaps using a mirror or asking a friend if he or she can recognise what you are trying to say.

Talk   Tell the congregation that instead of talking to them you are going to try instead to communicate without using words. Ask if anyone can tell what the following gestures mean:

Put finger to your lips	*Shush, be quiet*
Make beckoning gesture	*Come here*
Wave the back of your hands	*Go away*
Put hands up, palms forward	*Stop*
Shake fist	*I'll get you*
Cover both eyes with your hands	*How embarrassing*
Wagging finger	*Telling someone off*
Thumbs up	*Everything's OK*
Thumbs down	*It's no good/hasn't worked*
Scratch your head	*I'm thinking*
Yawn	*I'm tired*
Clap hands	*Applause*
Bow	*Taking the plaudits*
Hold up hands, palms a fraction apart	*It's this small*
Hold arms wide apart, palms turned in	*It's this big*
Put one finger in each ear	*Keep the noise down, you're deafening me*
Cup a hand behind your ear	*I can't hear you*
Place hand horizontally above eyes	*I can't quite see it; it's there somewhere*
Point a finger	*It's over there*
Shrug your shoulders	*I don't know, no idea*
Pretend to shake hands	*Hello, pleased to meet you*
Make circular motion with hand	*I'm slowing down (when driving)*

Punch the air with clenched fist/s	*I've won!*
Shake arm about in front of you	*Four runs* (cricket umpire's signal)
Raise outstretched hands to sky	*Six runs* (cricket umpire's signal)
Make an army salute	*Sir*

All of these illustrate that we can communicate powerfully without using words. In fact, a smile, wink, frown or glare can often say more than words can even begin to; hence the often-used expression 'actions speak louder than words'. Paradoxically, words can actually get in the way of communication, saying one thing while our actions say another. We might speak kindly while looking daggers at someone, preach kindness yet be the meanest person imaginable, talk of integrity but be dishonest in our dealings with others. All of which perhaps explains why the Bible has so much to say on the subject of our deeds marrying up with our words. 'Dear children,' we read in 1 John 3:18, 'let us not love with words or tongue but with actions and in truth.' Or, as James puts it (1:22; 2:17), 'Do not merely listen to the word, and so deceive yourselves. Do what it says . . . Faith by itself, if it is not accompanied by action, is dead.'

In other words, being a Christian means more than simply saying the right words. Yes, confession of faith is part of it, and no, God doesn't expect us to be perfect, but if we're serious about following Jesus, then something of him should show in our lives. According to Matthew, that 'something' should be a concern for others that makes itself visible through practical acts of caring, whether responding to the hungry, ensuring a supply of water for the thirsty, visiting the sick, providing clothes for those in need or responding to the persecuted. Through deeds such as these, faith shows itself in action. We may not have such needs on our doorstep, but there are numerous examples in the wider world – examples brought to our attention by such agencies as Christian Aid. In a world where the gulf between rich and poor grows ever wider, where millions go hungry and thirsty, and where nations still struggle with the burden of poverty and disease, the call to respond is as urgent as ever.

It's easy to talk about such things, to express dismay, to speak about the need for reform, and so on, but eventually it needs actions as well as words to change things, and it is actions rather than words that will testify to the reality of our faith. Do we respond meaningfully, generously, sacrificially to those in whose suffering Christ is crying out to us? Do we show through our actions that our concern for them is real? Actions speak louder than words; so what do your actions say to others about your faith?

FATHER'S DAY

53   Responding to the Father

Reading   Luke 15:11-32

Aim   To highlight the fatherly love of God, and to respond in praise and worship.

Preparation   On separate strips of card/paper, print the following lines of hymns. Ensure that the keywords highlighted in bold are roughly the same width by using larger letters where the word is short and small letters where it is long. If possible, highlight the keywords in a different colour. Avoid turnover lines if possible, but if any are needed ensure they do not overlap the keyword.

Dear Lord and Father of mankind

Father **God** I wonder how I managed to exist

We come unto **our** fathers' God

Great is thy faithfulness, O God my Father

Father whose mighty word, chaos **and** darkness heard

Lead us, **heavenly** Father, lead us

Eternal **Father**, strong to save

Father, hear the prayer **we** offer

Our Father God, thy name we **praise**

Abba Father, let me be yours, **and** yours alone

Father, we love you, we **worship** and adore you

Father, we adore **you**

For the might of your arm we bless you, our God, our fathers' God

Father, I place into **your** hands the things that I can't do

Of the Father's **love** begotten

Using pieces of blutack, stick up the hymn lines in prominent positions around the church. You will also need to enlist the help of your church organist or pianist for this talk. Give them a copy of the list of hymns, and prime them to play the first two lines of each as part of a *Name that tune* quiz during the talk.

Talk

Tell the congregation that you have something different for them today – a Father's Day version of the old musical quiz-show *Name that tune*. Explain that the organist/pianist is going to play the first lines of some well-known hymns and worship songs, all of which have the word 'Father' or 'fathers' in them. Their job is to identify the first line or lines of the hymn from the tune. As an extra clue, the various lines are displayed around the walls of the church.

Ask the organist/pianist, to play the first tune. If this is named correctly, ask if anyone can spot the line somewhere in the church. Invite whoever puts his or her hand up first to take it off the wall and bring it to you. Stick this on to a whiteboard, positioning it carefully as shown on pages 172-173. Continue in the same way for each of the various hymns, ensuring that the keyword in each hymn title lines up below the one above.

When each tune has been identified, thank the organist/pianist and all those who have helped you, and then read through the list of hymns again. Each one celebrates God as our Father or speaks of him as our fathers' God, and both of those ideas are appropriate themes for Father's Day. On the one hand, we are here to think of fathers, to remember all we owe to them and to express our appreciation of all they mean or once meant to us. This is a day that calls fathers to consider their responsibilities, and children to consider their response.

It is impossible, though, to think of fathers without also thinking of 'Our Father': as Jesus encouraged us to picture God. Throughout the Scriptures we find him described in this way, and perhaps nowhere is what that means better illustrated than in the parable Jesus told of the lost or prodigal son. We call it that, but, as many have observed, the parable is as much about the father as the son; the father who, it seems, looks out longingly each day in the hope of seeing his child returning, and who, when he does this, runs out with open arms to greet him and welcome him home.

That's the God we serve: not stern, remote and forbidding, but full of love, yearning to draw us close, always ready to forgive and forget, constantly looking to restore our relationship with him however often we might break it. Ours is a God who guides, loves, saves and protects, faithfully watching over us, his nature always to have mercy. That's why so many of the hymns and songs we sing today acknowledge him as Father, and that's what these hymns we've identified today are all about. But, as you've probably already spotted, this particular selection has one more thing to say to us as well. (Ask someone to read the highlighted words, from top to bottom.) 'Dear God our Great and heavenly Father, we praise and worship you For your love.' A simple prayer through which we can respond and express our gratitude for all God has done for us. (Finish the talk by inviting the congregation to join with you in saying the prayer together. See next two pages.)

Dear Lord and Father of
mankind

Father **God** I wonder how I
managed to exist

We come unto **our** fathers' God

Great is thy faithfulness, O God
my Father

Father whose mighty word, chaos **and** darkness heard

Lead us, **heavenly** Father, lead us

Eternal **Father**, strong to save

Father, hear the prayer we offer

Our Father God, thy name we **praise**

Abba Father, let me be yours, **and** yours alone

Father, we love you, we **worship** and adore you

Father, we adore you

For the might of your arm we bless you, our God, our fathers' God

Father, I place into **your** hands the things that I can't do

Of the Father's **love** begotten

54   The Father of all

Readings

Ephesians 4:1-6; Romans 8:12-17

Aim

To celebrate the part fathers play in our lives and to recognise that God is the Father of all.

Preparation

Print on individual pieces of card/paper the letters in the word-search below and arrange them carefully on a whiteboard as shown. Fix them with a single small piece of blutack so that they can be removed easily during the talk.

N	W	O	R	B	T	T	R	S	H	E	G
R	C	N	A	M	I	E	E	R	Y	I	R
M	H	E	S	O	M	N	H	E	M	E	A
A	R	G	S	O	E	R	T	H	R	M	N
I	I	S	D	U	A	A	A	T	A	A	D
L	S	N	A	G	O	D	F	A	F	H	F
L	T	G	U	U	A	H	D	F	D	A	A
I	M	S	I	T	C	H	O	E	A	R	T
W	A	E	R	B	O	E	G	R	Y	B	H
F	S	S	E	M	A	H	T	O	A	A	E
L	O	N	G	L	E	G	S	F	L	L	R

Talk

Tell the congregation that you have a simple combined quiz and word-search for them. All the questions/clues are concerned with dads or fathers, and the answers (given in italics) point to the words hidden in the word-search. (The words to look for in the latter are highlighted in capitals.) As each answer is given and subsequently found in the word-search, remove the appropriate letters of the word from the board and discard them. The clues are as follows:

• A personification of the passing of the years: *Old Father TIME*

• 'You are old, Father _____', the young man said: *WILLIAM*

• Another name for the second-longest river in Britain: *Old Father THAMES*

• A venerable Smurf: *Father ABRAHAM*

- A priest-cum-detective created by G. K. Chesterton: *Father BROWN*
- This well-loved character is associated with a special season: *Father CHRISTMAS*
- The name given to the longest serving member in the House of Commons: *Father of the HOUSE*
- According to Wordsworth, 'the child is _____': *father of the MAN*
- Another name for our ancestors: *FOREFATHERS*
- A large old-fashioned timepiece: *GRANDFATHER clock*
- Either a male sponsor at a child's baptism or the head of a mafia gang: *GODFATHER*
- The name given to the Home Guard during the Second World War: *Dad's ARMY*
- Another name for the crane fly and the harvestman: *Daddy-LONG-LEGS*
- A one-time larger-than-life wrestler: *BIG Daddy*
- The name given to a middle-aged or elderly man who showers gifts on a much younger woman: *SUGAR Daddy*
- A popular and flavoursome accompaniment to food: *Dad's SAUCE*
- The occasion we're here to celebrate: *Father's DAY*

At the end of the talk, all that should be left on the board is this:

						T			H	E		
R						E				I		
			S	O		N				E		
		G		O								
			D			A						
		N				D			F			
				A								
			T		H							
		E	R		O							
F									A			
									L	L		

Ask if anyone in the congregation can read what the remaining letters spell, reading from left to right, top to bottom. After someone has identified the text, close up the letters to spell it out more clearly: 'There is one God and Father of all' (Ephesians 4:4a, 6a).

We are here today, of course, to give thanks for fathers – for all they mean or have meant to us – but we are here also to remember the One who is the Father of all, and to give thanks for the love, goodness, grace and mercy he shows to us each day. Don't forget what fathers do. Make a point of showing your appreciation, whenever and wherever you can. Equally, don't forget what God does, what God means, what God has given – and, in turn, show him, through words and deeds, how grateful you are.

HARVEST

55   Gifts of the world

Reading   Psalm 104:1-30

Aim   To bring home the global dimension of Harvest, and to stress the importance of all enjoying a share in what God has given.

Preparation   Print the following in large bold letters on separate slips of paper/card:

HAWAII, SRI LANKA, ITALY, TURKEY, CHINA, BRAZIL, SAUDI ARABIA, NEW ZEALAND, FRANCE, SOUTH AFRICA, SPAIN, WEST INDIES, SCOTLAND, ORANGES, FIGS, HAGGIS, PINEAPPLES, KIWI FRUIT, OIL, WINE, TEA, COFFEE, PASTA, RICE, DIAMONDS, BANANAS

Attach a small piece of magnetic tape or blutack to the back of each slip and arrange them at random on a whiteboard.

Talk   Ask if people can identify matching pairs from the words on the display board. The pairs are as follows:

HAWAII	PINEAPPLES
SRI LANKA	TEA
ITALY	PASTA
TURKEY	FIGS
CHINA	RICE
BRAZIL	COFFEE
SAUDI ARABIA	OIL
NEW ZEALAND	KIWI FRUIT
FRANCE	WINE
SOUTH AFRICA	DIAMONDS
SPAIN	ORANGES
WEST INDIES	BANANAS
SCOTLAND	HAGGIS

Of course, many of these items are grown in places other than the one shown, and many of these countries grow different crops, but this short list provides an important reminder that when we think of and celebrate Harvest today we are talking not just about a local harvest but also about the wider world. Look at the label next time you eat something, and see where it was grown or produced. Apples from South Africa, tea from Sri Lanka, butter from New Zealand – the food we eat derives from various continents, and our modern-day harvest has a global dimension that we cannot and must not ignore.

We are part of a wider world in which countries, people and economies are interdependent.

Harvest, then, is a time for celebrating God's creation and giving thanks for the food and plenty we enjoy, but it is a time also for remembering the contribution and needs of others and for resolving to work, so far as we are able, towards a world in which all have a fair share in God's abundant harvest.

56 A hidden Harvest message

Reading

Psalm 65:1, 9-13

Aim

To bring home the fact that Harvest involves human effort that should be appreciated but that it is finally dependent on God.

Preparation

On separate pieces of card or paper, print the following in large bold letters:

TURNIP, HERBS, APPLE, NUTS, KIWI FRUIT, GRAPES, ONION, DAMSON, FLOWERS, ORANGE, RHUBARB, AUBERGINE, LEMON, LEEK

Attach a piece of blutack or magnetic tape to the back of each, and retain for use during the talk. Ensure you have them in order, so that you are not rummaging around to find the correct word during the talk.

If possible, arrange for one of each of these to be on display as part of the Harvest produce, ready for you to use as a visual aid. If this is not possible, make a simple line drawing of each fruit and vegetable etc. instead. You will also need some tins and packets of brand-labelled products that can be readily identified by members of the congregation – for example, Walkers crisps, Jacob's cream crackers, Heinz baked beans, HP spaghetti, Princes pineapple pieces, McDougalls flour, Mr Kipling's cakes, John West tuna, KP peanuts, Robertson's jam, Fray Bentos corned beef.

Talk

Hold up each of the brand-labelled products and ask what it is and who made it. The congregation should have little difficulty in identifying each item and its 'manufacturer'. You could be forgiven for thinking, reading the labels, that these products are all man-made, and in a sense they are, because the ingredients within them have been grown or reared by farmers or trawled by fishermen and then processed, canned or so forth by various manufacturers and packagers. All sorts of people are involved in providing the food we put on our tables, and a proper celebration of Harvest needs to involve a recognition of and thanksgiving for all the work that goes into its production.

But of course, although these products have needed some input, none of them is truly man-made. To illustrate what I mean, identify the following (hold up the fruits and vegetables etc. listed overleaf) and as each is identified, place the matching word on a whiteboard in a column, as shown).

TURNIP
HERBS
APPLE
NUTS
KIWI FRUIT

GRAPES
ONION
DAMSON

FLOWERS
ORANGE
RHUBARB

AUBERGINE
LEMON
LEEK

Ask if anybody can see the message that these fruits, nuts and vegetables convey. The answer, of course, is spelt out by reading the first letter of every word downwards: THANK GOD FOR ALL! This is what Harvest is ultimately all about; it reminds us that although human hands play a very real part in producing the things we eat, God is ultimately the provider and maker of all. Give thanks, then, today for all behind our Harvest, but above all, give thanks to him who makes it all possible.

57 Looking into Harvest

Readings Psalm 145 (various Bible verses are also included as part of this talk)

Aim To explore the various aspects of what Harvest has to say to us today.

Preparation On separate squares of card, one per letter, print in large bold print the word HARVEST, seven times. Fasten magnetic tape or blutack to the back of each letter, and then arrange on a whiteboard to spell the word HARVEST seven times in a column down the left side.

Next, print the following Bible verses (own translation) on large strips of paper, and display in prominent positions around the church:

- The earth has produced its harvest. God, our God, has blessed us! (Psalm 67:6)
- You will have more than enough to eat, and be well satisfied. (Joel 2:26)
- My father's hired hands have food in plenty but here am I about to starve. (Luke 15:17).
- They called for help, but nobody was there to save them. (Psalm 18:41)
- God is able to supply you with good things in profusion, so that, invariably having sufficient of everything, you may share lavishly in good works of every kind. (2 Corinthians 9:8)

Talk Point to the board and tell the congregation that there are no prizes for guessing what you want to talk about: HARVEST! Ask if anyone can think of words we might make out of the letters spelling 'Harvest'. There are numerous possibilities – for example, HEART, VEST, EARS, TEAR, TEA, THE, HAS and STAR. Continue taking suggestions until the ideas start to run short, then tell the congregation that you want to focus on six words (which may have been mentioned or not). The words can be found in the six verses positioned around the church. Read the first verse: 'The earth has produced its harvest. God, our God, has blessed us!' (Psalm 67:6), and ask if anyone can spot the word in question: EARTH. (As each word is correctly identified in the verses, remove the letters from the next complete 'HARVEST' on the board, and rearrange the letters to spell the new word.)

'Earth' could hardly be a more fitting word in relation to Harvest for both its meanings are central to thanksgiving. 'Earth' can mean the soil in which we grow things, providing the vital moisture, minerals and nutrients on which all growth depends. It can also mean the planet on which we live, with all its beauty and variety, wonder and mystery. It is here that Harvest begins: in celebrating the world God has given to us, the life it sustains and the fruitfulness it exhibits.

What about the second of our verses: 'You will have more than enough to eat, and be well satisfied' (Joel 2:26)? The word this time is EAT: and once more this takes us to what Harvest is traditionally all about: a celebration of what God has given us to eat, of the food we enjoy. The fruit, vegetables and other foodstuffs with which we decorate our churches at Harvest represent just a small selection of the good things we eat by God's grace.

But let's go on a bit further, to our third verse: 'My father's hired hands have food in plenty but here am I about to starve' (Luke 15:17). There are two words here that we might make from Harvest: one is HAVE and the other is STARVE. The word 'have' reminds us of what Harvest can too easily become: a celebration of our good fortune whilst forgetting the needs of others. We are those who *have*; even the poorest of us are rich and affluent compared with the hungry of so many in our world. Even while we give thanks now for another rich harvest, thousands today will be starving, millions denied a just reward for their labours or facing another failed harvest and famine.

All of which leads us on to our next verse: 'They called for help, but nobody was there to save them' (Psalm 18:41). The word this time is SAVE, which again can be taken in two ways. We all like to save money, and many of us will probably look in the shops for the best bargains, but sometimes when it comes to buying food or things such as tea and coffee we have to balance saving money with perhaps paying that little extra for fair-trade goods; goods for which those who grew or produced them receive fair payment. Through doing that we can do something, if only a little, to help save some from the horrors of poverty, hunger, oppression and exploitation.

This leads us finally to the last verse: 'God is able to supply you with good things in profusion, so that, invariably having sufficient of everything, you may share lavishly in good works of every kind' (2 Corinthians 9:8). The word here is SHARE, and again it is central to a proper celebration of Harvest, for this should not just be a time for ourselves, enjoying all God has given us, but a time when, recognising how fortunate we are and how much we've been given, we share with others, giving from our plenty to help those who have less.

EARTH, EAT, HAVE, STARVE, SAVE, SHARE: all are part of the true meaning of Harvest and we need to consider the meaning and challenge of each one if we are truly to understand and celebrate what Harvest is all about.

ONE WORLD WEEK

58   All God's people

Readings   Romans 10:5-13; Galatians 3:23-29

Aim   To emphasise that in God's eyes we are all individuals of equal worth, no matter what our colour, culture or creed.

Preparation   Copy and enlarge the following map of the world, or, if preferred, use a copy of your own (a large colour map will make more of a visual impression). Stick this at the front of the church on a wall or display board in a position that is clearly visible to all. (If using your own map, you will need to add the numbers 1-20 as shown.)

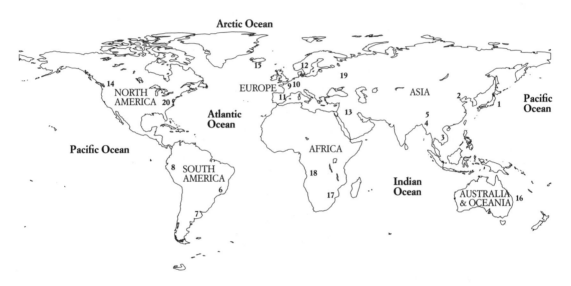

The World

In large bold letters, print the following on separate strips of paper/card:

TOKYO, BEIJING, BANGKOK, CALCUTTA, KATHMANDU, RIO DE JANEIRO, BUENOS AIRES, LIMA, CALAIS, BERLIN, BARCELONA, OSLO, BAGHDAD, VANCOUVER, REYKJAVIK, SYDNEY, PRETORIA, KINSHASA, MOSCOW, NEW YORK, IRAQI, GERMAN, CHINESE, BRAZILIAN, FRENCH, NORWEGIAN, THAI, JAPANESE, AUSTRALIAN, ARGENTINIAN, INDIAN, PERUVIAN, SPANISH, NEPALESE, CANADIAN, AMERICAN, ZAIRIAN, SOUTH AFRICAN, RUSSIAN, ICELANDIC.

Display in prominent positions around the church.

Talk   Tell the congregation that since it's One World Week you have prepared a quiz for them about countries and people of the world. All they have to do is identify the country in which each place you name is found, and the nationality of someone from there. After each correct answer (given in italics after the place), ask if anyone can spot the place name and the corresponding nationality displayed somewhere in the church. Ask whoever finds these to bring them to you, and stick each place name in the appropriate position on the board (see the number in parentheses following each country) displaying the nationality below this.

a. KINSHASA (18): ZAIRE, *ZAIRIAN*

b. BARCELONA (11): SPAIN, *SPANISH*

c. LIMA (8): PERU, *PERUVIAN*

d. CALCUTTA (4): INDIA, *INDIAN*

e. REYKJAVIK (15): ICELAND, *ICELANDIC*

f. TOKYO (1): JAPAN, *JAPANESE*

g. OSLO (12): NORWAY, *NORWEGIAN*

h. PRETORIA (17): SOUTH AFRICA: *SOUTH AFRICAN*

i. BEIJING (2): CHINA, *CHINESE*

j. KATHMANDU (5): NEPAL, *NEPALESE*

k. SYDNEY (16): AUSTRALIA, *AUSTRALIAN*

l. BERLIN (10): GERMANY, *GERMAN*

m. MOSCOW (19): RUSSIA, *RUSSIAN*

n. BUENOS AIRES (7): ARGENTINA, *ARGENTINIAN*

o. NEW YORK (20): USA, *AMERICAN*

p. RIO DE JANEIRO (6): BRAZIL, *BRAZILIAN*

q. CALAIS (9): FRANCE, *FRENCH*

r. BAGHDAD (13): IRAQ, *IRAQI*

s. BANGKOK (3): THAILAND, *THAI*

t. VANCOUVER (14): CANADA, *CANADIAN*

These are just some of the places, countries and nationalities from across the world, all part of a bewildering variety representing a host of colours and creeds and cultures. They are what make this world such a fascinating place, but they are also, sadly, what so often lead to division, the differences between us leading to suspicion, hatred, war and violence.

Such divisions were there, equally, in biblical times, and in the early Church, which, in its early days, wrestled with the question of the relationship between Jews and Gentiles – those who followed the Law of Moses and those outside it. Could non-Jews become Christians, accepted as God's people? Had the Church outgrown Judaism, or did the teaching of the Jewish Law still need to be followed?

For the Apostle Paul there was no question as to the answer. Whatever divides us is as nothing compared to what unites us. God's love is for all, not just the few. So strongly did he feel about this that he drove home his message in three separate letters. First, to the Galatians (3:28), he writes, 'There is no longer Jew or Greek, there is no longer slave or free, there is no longer male and female; for all of you are one in Christ Jesus.' Or as he put it to the Romans (10:11-13, own translation), 'As it says in scripture, "No one who puts their faith in him will be put to shame." For there is no differentiation between Jew and Greek; the same Lord is Lord of all and generous to all those who call on him. As it says again, "Everyone who calls on the name of the Lord will be saved."' Finally, there are Paul's words to the Colossians (3:11): 'There is no longer Greek and Jew, circumcised and uncircumcised, barbarian, Scythian, slave and free; but Christ is all and in all.' That doesn't, of course, do away with our differences overnight, nor does it say that we accept every view, creed or practice of those in other cultures, but it does mean that we should respect our common humanity, recognising that all are important to God, whoever they are, wherever they come from.

We live today, as people have lived throughout history, in a broken and divided world, racked by tensions and problems to which we see no easy answers. Yet it is, above all, God's world, created by and precious to him. So today we pray again for unity, for peace among nations, and for the time when it will be one world not just in name but in truth.

59 One world

Readings

Genesis 11:1-9; John 17:1-26

Aim

To illustrate the fact that we are all one in our common humanity, and that God longs for the day when the things that divide us will be overcome so that we may truly live as one.

Preparation

Cut a large circle out of a piece of thick card, to represent the world. Make a hole in the centre sufficiently large for the circle to spin easily once it has been loosely but securely pinned to a board. Cut a second circle of the same size out of a thinner piece of card and cut this into twelve equal-sized quadrants. Colour four of these red, four blue, and four yellow. (Alternatively, you may choose to cut four quadrants each out of red, blue and yellow card.) In large bold letters, label the quadrants as follows:

AFRICA, ANTARCTICA, EUROPE, ASIA, SOUTH AMERICA, NORTH AMERICA, AUSTRALIA, EAST, WEST, NORTH, SOUTH, THIRD WORLD

Attach pieces of blutack to the back of these so that they can be firmly attached during the talk to the circle representing the world. Pin the latter to a board, as described above.

Talk

Tell the congregation that you have some very simple questions to ask them about the world. First, how many continents are there? The answer, of course, is seven. What are these? As each is called out – Africa, Antarctica, Europe, Asia, South America, North America and Australia – stick the appropriate quadrant on to the circle so that one butts up against another. What two directional terms were generally used to describe the 'protagonists' in the so-called Cold War? (East and West; again, attach these quadrants to the circle.) Which two directions are typically used to describe the rich and poor hemispheres of the world? (North and South; once more, attach quadrants.) Finally, what term is often used to describe the poor and underdeveloped regions of the world? (Third World; attach the final quadrant.)

These various terms in different ways cover the nations and people of our planet, just as the colours we've used to represent them can be used to cover every colour in the spectrum. Ask what they are called (primary colours). What colour, for example, will blue and yellow make (green)? What will yellow and red make (orange)? What will red and blue make (purple)? And so on. But primary colours have one other fascinating and important feature, a feature which points to something equally fascinating and important about people.

(Spin the circle round as fast as you can make it go. The colours will merge to make white.) The various colours go together to make a single colour; what seemed divided becomes one.

The book of Genesis paints a picture of an idealised world when all were one, in the sense that people spoke the same language, but speaks also of the breakdown of that unity, people scattered across the earth into different nations, cultures and tongues; differences that have shown themselves in tensions and divisions across history. Such tension and division are not what God wants, as the prayer of Jesus recorded in John 17 makes plain. Having prayed for his followers and for the Church, he moves on to pray for unity in the world, for a time when all people will be united through him. That prayer reminds us that Jesus died not simply for a few but for all; that God does not just love the Church but also and equally loves the world. We share a common humanity; on that, irrespective of faith, we need to build. Today, then, we remember that, above all, this is God's world, and in that conviction we commit ourselves to, as best we can, seeking, praying for and working towards one world.

60   God's world

Readings   Psalm 24; John 3:13-21

Aim   To bring home that God's love and purpose extends to the whole world.

Preparation   On separate strips of paper/card, print the following in large bold letters:

> JAPAN, EUROPE, SOUTH AMERICA, UNITED STATES, SOUTH AFRICA, SWEDEN, AUSTRALIA, INDIA, DENMARK, ISRAEL, AFRICA, MEXICO, TURKEY, HONG KONG, EGYPT, LAPLAND, ICELAND, GERMANY, HOLLAND, THAILAND, OSLO, FRANCE, TANZANIA, HUNGARY, ETHIOPIA, WEST INDIES, OMAN, RUSSIA, LIECHTENSTEIN, DOMINICAN REPUBLIC

Attach blutack or magnetic tape to the back of each and retain in the order printed, ready for use later in the talk.

For the clues marked 'Shape' below, trace the shape of the country or continent in question on to a piece of coloured card and then cut this out, ready to display during the talk as a clue.

Talk   Tell the congregation that, in keeping with One World Sunday, you have prepared a geographical quiz. Most of the answers are countries or continents; a few relate to provinces, principalities, capital cities and suchlike. As each correct answer is given, stick the matching word on to a display board, using one to two columns as necessary, as shown beneath the quiz clues below:

1. The capital of this country is Tokyo (JAPAN)
2. France, Holland and the UK are all part of this continent (EUROPE)
3. Shape: (SOUTH AMERICA)
4. George Washington was once President of this country (UNITED STATES)
5. A country that was formerly separated by apartheid (SOUTH AFRICA)
6. The home country of Sven Goran Eriksson (SWEDEN)
7. Shape: (AUSTRALIA)
8. The Taj Mahal can be found here (INDIA)
9. A place perhaps where you might expect to find a Great Dane? (DENMARK)
10. A country in which most of Old Testament is set (ISRAEL)

11. Shape: (AFRICA)

12. A country in Central America where people wear sombreros (MEXICO)

13. A country which sounds like a bird eaten at Christmas (TURKEY)

14. A province handed back to China in 1997 (HONG KONG)

15. Land of the Pharaohs (EGYPT)

16. Reputedly the home of Father Christmas (LAPLAND)

17. This sounds like a very cold country (ICELAND)

18. This country used to be divided by the Berlin Wall (GERMANY)

19. A flat country famous for its tulips and dykes (HOLLAND)

20. Bangkok is the capital of this country (THAILAND)

21. The capital of Norway (OSLO)

22. The nearest Continental country to England (FRANCE)

23. Mount Kilimanjaro is on this country's border with Kenya (TANZANIA)

24. A country that sounds in need of food (HUNGARY)

25. An African country plagued by famine (ETHIOPIA)

26. Another name for the Caribbean, this region is famed for its Test Cricket teams (WEST INDIES)

27. An oil-producing country in the Middle East (OMAN)

28. A country that used to be at the heart of the old Soviet Union (RUSSIA)

29. A tiny principality in central Europe (LIECHTENSTEIN)

30. A country in the Caribbean, famed for its production of coffee, cocoa and bananas (DOMINICAN REPUBLIC)

JAPAN
EUROPE
SOUTH AMERICA
UNITED STATES
SOUTH AFRICA

SWEDEN
AUSTRALIA
INDIA
DENMARK

ISRAEL

AFRICA
MEXICO

TURKEY
HONG KONG
EGYPT

LAPLAND
ICELAND
GERMANY
HOLLAND
THAILAND

OSLO
FRANCE

TANZANIA
HUNGARY
ETHIOPIA

WEST INDIES
OMAN
RUSSIA
LIECHTENSTEIN
DOMINICAN REPUBLIC

These are just some of the numerous countries and places in our world, together representing an astonishing variety of creeds, colours, cultures and customs. They remind us that our own country is but one tiny part of the wider world, a world that is all important and precious to God, part of his plans. Ask if anyone can see evidence of that truth hidden in our list of countries, i.e. 'Jesus said, "I am the light of the world"' (John 8:12), spelt out by reading the first letter of each word.

God wants us to remember that just as all people are his concern so they are ours to. We have a responsibility to other nations, in terms of economic and environmental issues, as well as in our prayers and in supporting the work of mission. We have something to give but also something to receive, each of us part of the family of humankind. Thank God for our world, but above all, never forget it is *his* world first.

REMEMBRANCE
SUNDAY

61   Let's grow feet!

Readings   Deuteronomy 6:4-9; Luke 22:14-23

Aim   To emphasise the importance of remembering those who gave their lives in the two World Wars and subsequent conflicts, and to illustrate how Remembrance Sunday and Remembrance Day help us do just that.

Preparation   On separate squares of card, one per letter, print the following, in large bold letters:

L G F E R E T O E S W T

Fasten blutack or magnetic tape to the *front and back* of each letter, and retain for use during the talk.

Talk   Tell the congregation that you want to test their memory today. Hold up the lettered 'cards' you have prepared and announce that you want people to remember where you put them. Place the cards, face down, on a whiteboard, as below, announcing each letter as you do so, starting at the bottom right-hand corner and working upwards so as not to give the game away (the letter is shown in outline on each square, though of course this will not be seen by the congregation):

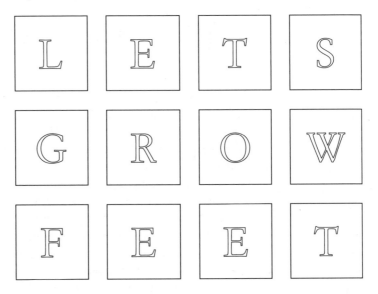

Ask if anyone can tell you where an O is. How about a G, an F, an E, an S and so forth (the chances are that very few people will guess correctly). Continue until you feel the congregation have had enough. Now announce that you are going to make things a lot easier. Carefully reposition the letters, face downwards, so that they again spell out the message LETS / GROW / FEET, but this time tell the congregation what you have done. Ask if someone can find you the letter O now, and so on (turn over each letter as it is correctly identified). The congregation should have no problem in matching every letter on the board.

Remembering isn't always easy. With the best will in the world, we can forget even important things. That's why we invent tools, like knots in a hankie, memo boards and mnemonics to help us remember, and that, of course, is what we've done in our puzzle today. Not that there's much point in remembering the words LETS GROW FEET, unless we're playing a memory game, but the letters can easily be rearranged into an infinitely more important message. Arrange the letters on the whiteboard, as follows:

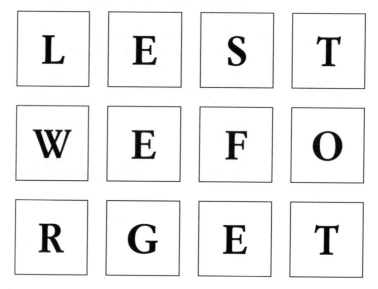

The message now is clear enough: words central to this day and to Remembrance Day itself. Many will be wearing poppies, some will listen to the sounding of the Last Post or the firing of a salute, some will repeat the words 'We will remember them' after the equally familiar lines 'They shall not grow old, as we that are left grow old. Age shall not weary them, nor the years condemn. At the going down of the sun and in the morning, we will remember them.'

Why do we do such things? Simply, but vitally, to remember those who gave their lives for us, and those who continue to give their lives in the armed forces today. We do this, lest we forget; because the lessons of the past are too important to be forgotten.

It is many years now since the last World War ended, and there are fewer and fewer people old enough to remember first-hand what happened. But, just as the Jews were told in the book of Deuteronomy to bind the words of the Law as an emblem to their foreheads and write them on the doorposts of their houses, so we need to remember the cost of war and the price of peace, LEST WE FORGET.

62 Remembering and learning

Readings   Various readings are included as part of this talk.

Aim   This talk, like the last one, uses the idea of a memory game, but this time the emphasis is on learning from what's gone before; an idea which is subsequently expanded in terms of learning what God has done for us and from the sacrifice of those who have given their lives in war.

Preparation   On separate squares of card, one per letter, print two sets of the following, in large bold letters:

TITNODTERGOF

Fasten blutack or magnetic tape to the *front and back* of each letter, and arrange these face down on a whiteboard, as follows (the letter is shown in outline on each square, though of course this will not be seen by the participants):

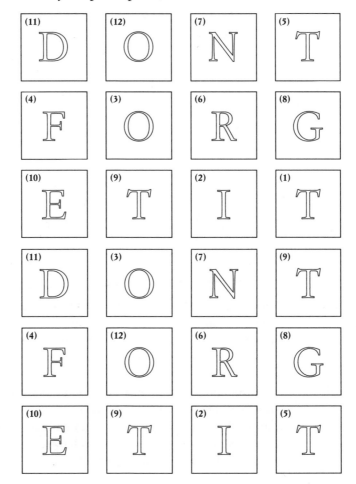

Next, on separate slips of paper but in normal print size, print off the following Bible verses:

(1) Deuteronomy 4:9a: 'But take care and watch yourselves closely, so as neither to forget the things that your eyes have seen nor to let them slip from your mind all the days of your life.'

(2) Deuteronomy 4:23a: 'So be careful not to forget the covenant that the Lord your God made with you.'

(3) Deuteronomy 8:11a: 'Take care that you do not forget the Lord your God, by failing to keep his commandments, his ordinances, and his statutes.'

(4) Psalm 103:2: 'Bless the Lord, O my soul, and do not forget all his benefits.'

(5) Psalm 106:10, 13a, 21: 'So he saved them from the hand of the foe, and delivered them from the hand of the enemy . . . But they soon forgot his works . . . They forgot God, their Saviour, who had done great things for them in Egypt.'

(6) Psalm 119:83b, 93, 109b: 'I have not forgotten your statutes . . . I will never forget your precepts, for by them you have given me life . . . I do not forget your law.'

(7) Proverbs 4:5: 'Get wisdom; get insight: do not forget, nor turn away.'

(8) Proverbs 3:1: 'My child, do not forget my teaching, but let your heart keep my commandments.'

(9) Jeremiah 3:21: 'A voice on the bare heights is heard, the plaintive weeping of Israel's children, because they have perverted their way, they have forgotten the Lord their God.'

(10) James 1:25: 'But those who look into the perfect law . . . being not hearers who forget but doers who act – they will be blessed in their doing.'

(11) Jeremiah 2:32b: 'Yet my people have forgotten me, days without number.'

(12) Isaiah 51:13a: 'You have forgotten the Lord your Maker, who stretched out the heavens and laid the foundations of the earth.'

Distribute these to members of the congregation prior to the talk/service, making sure that they know which number reading theirs is, and prime them to read the verse when the corresponding pair of numbers comes up during the talk.

Talk   Tell the congregation that you have prepared a memory game and ask for three volunteers to take part. The aim of the game is very simple: in two guesses to find two letters that match. However, since there are more than two of some letters, each square has also been numbered, participants need to find letters for which the numbers also match. When a matching pair is found, place these face upwards on the board in the same positions from which they were taken, and ask whoever has the reading with corresponding number to stand up and read his or her verse (it may be as well to repeat the verse afterwards, for the benefit of those who are hard of hearing). Continue until all the letters on the board have been overturned.

The game is fairly straightforward, but it has an important lesson, which of course we can see spelt out now and repeated on the board: DON'T FORGET IT! We need to learn from what has happened if we hope to get things right next time. That is the message equally in each of our Bible verses: remember what God has done, is the constant refrain, often addressed to those who have failed to do that, forgetting his love and turning their backs on his will.

The message, of course, is hugely appropriate for Remembrance Sunday and Remembrance Day itself. We do not simply look back and remember for the sake of it, but with a view to learning the lessons of the past, so that if possible peace can be preserved but if necessary evil is confronted before it is allowed to get out of hand.

Don't forget all you owe to God; don't forget all you owe to others: remember, learn and apply the lessons for today.

CHURCH
ANNIVERSARY

63   Building bricks

Readings   Ephesians 2:1-22; 1 Peter 2:1-10

Aim   To stress that the health and future of any church depends on how far its life and witness are based on Christ.

Preparation   For this talk, you will need 12 small plastic flowerpots, a pack of playing cards, and nine household bricks with which to build a mini-church building. Construct a 'building' out of playing cards by laying them edge up against each other, laying cards flat on top of these, and subsequently adding other 'storeys' of cards. The resulting edifice will be very unstable, so take care not to disturb it and be prepared, if necessary, to rebuild it swiftly.

Arrange the flowerpots into a 'pyramid wall', five pots in a row at the base, four pots balanced on these, and three more balanced on these.

Finally, attach a large sticky label to each brick, turning five on end, and label them as illustrated below.

PEACE	SERVICE

FELLOWSHIP	WORSHIP

C H R I S T	F A I T H	H O P E	G R A C E	P R A Y E R

Stack the bricks into a wall comprising three rows of three, with the words facing away from the congregation (again, see below). If you erect the wall on a communion table, be sure to cover this first with a thick blanket to prevent any damage.

Talk   Ask how many people remember the story of 'The Three Little Pigs', and then ask if anyone can remember what happens in the story. Tell the congregation that with their help you're going to re-enact that story in your talk, and ask for three volunteers to have a go at blowing your walls down.

Invite your first volunteer to blow down the playing-card building. It should collapse almost immediately. Invite your second volunteer to blow down the flowerpot wall. This will probably collapse as easily as the first. Ask your final volunteer to blow down the brick wall. They will, of course, have no chance whatsoever!

The reason, obviously, is that, unlike the playing cards and flower-pots, the bricks are strong and heavy, built to last. And there's a lesson in all this concerning the Church. For a church to last and be strong, it needs to be built of the right materials; not bricks, but other equally important building blocks. Turn the bricks round, recon-structing them so that the labels face the congregation, as follows:

P R A Y E R	G R A C E			
C H R I S T	F A I T H	FELLOWSHIP	SERVICE	H O P E
		WORSHIP	PEACE	

These are the building blocks of the Church, whether this or any other fellowship. The cornerstone, of course, is *Christ*. Alongside this we need *faith*, a faith that shows itself both in *prayer* and *worship* and also in *service*. We need time to share *fellowship*, living in *peace* with one another. We need to be a people of *hope*, trusting in what God is doing and is going to do among us, and confident also of his eternal purpose for us and all his people. We cannot, though, make all that happen ourselves; we depend finally on his *grace* to take and shape us into the church he wants us to be.

You may be wondering about one final thing. What binds these building blocks together? With real bricks, of course, we'd use cement, but with the Church, it's different: the final thing needed is love.

We are here today to celebrate another chapter in the life of this church, and to look forward to what we hope will be many more chapters to come. How many there will be, and what will be written in them, depends on how far these things are part of our life together; how far these are the building blocks through which Christ can continue to build his church here in this place.

64   <u>What the Church can become</u>

Readings   John 17:20-23; Ephesians 2:11-22

Aim   To explore what, by God's grace, the Church is (or should be) always in the process of becoming.

Preparation   Print (to scale and in as large letters as possible) the following letters:

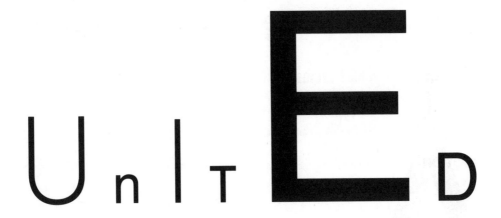

Fasten magnetic tape or blutack to the back of each, and arrange the letters as on the next page.

Talk   Point to the 'picture' you have prepared and ask what it represents. The congregation will rightly observe that it portrays a church. Agree, but remind them of the often-repeated saying that the Church is the people, not the building. Proceed to illustrate that by separating the letters into the following four words:

OPEN
CARING
UNITED
CHURCH

Here is the goal that every church should set itself: of being an open, caring and united church – open to all, whoever they may be; caring for all within the fellowship; and united in faith and vision, both in terms of the immediate family and the wider family of the Church.

We never, of course, reach perfection, and often fall well short of that ideal, but as we come today to celebrate another year in the life of this fellowship, let us consider what God is constantly striving to help us become, and so commit ourselves to being more truly the church he would have us be.

65 Names from the past

Reading Hebrews 13:7-8

Aim This talk – suitable only for those churches that have commemoratory plaques around the church or items such as tables, books, chairs dedicated to individuals – emphasises the debt we owe to the past and the fact that we have a responsibility to present and future generations.

Preparation The only preparation needed for this talk is to look round the various plaques/dedications within your church and to prepare a list of questions concerning these – for example: Who died in [year]? Who gave the [item/s] to this church and in memory of whom? Who served as [position] in this church from [dates]? Who founded this church? Tailor the questions to reflect the wording of dedications, so as to give clues to the identity of each individual.

Talk Tell the congregation that since they are celebrating an anniversary, you have prepared a quiz concerning the past history of the church. Ask the various questions you have prepared.

All of these people – some known personally to us, some just names – represent those who have been part of this church, serving God in their own different ways within it. They are part of the story of this fellowship, part of *our* story. We tread in their footsteps, carrying on the work they were part of, and if we would truly honour their names, then we will do our utmost to take forward the life and witness of this church so that future generations may be part of its story in turn. We may not have plaques or memorials erected to remember us, but out legacy will be having helped build for the future in the service of Christ, the same yesterday, today and tomorrow.

CHURCH
MEMBERSHIP

66   Joined together in Christ

Readings   Matthew 18:20; Colossians 2:1-6

Aim   To emphasise the need for fellowship in and commitment to the life of the Church.

Preparation   On a large sheet of paper, or a whiteboard, prepare a join-the-dots picture of a church building, such as the one in the illustration below. If possible, make the dots light enough not to be seen from a distance. You may wish to copy and enlarge the example below (a larger version may be found in the Photocopy Masters section on page 312), or you may prefer instead to create your own design. If you choose the latter option, make sure that you number the dots, so that volunteers are able to follow the dots correctly. Fix the 'picture' to a board and place it in a prominent but accessible position at the front of the church.

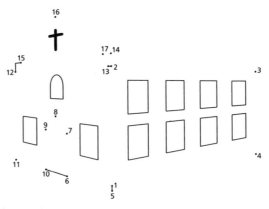

Talk   Display the 'join-the-dots' picture, and ask if anyone can identify what it portrays. It's unlikely that anyone will be able to do so. Ask a young person (or people) to come forward and help join the dots. Supervise this carefully, to make sure that they complete the picture correctly! Continue until the picture of the church building is revealed.

While you can just make out the image from the various dots if you look hard enough, it's only when the dots are joined together that the full picture becomes clear. The same is true of the Church as a people. It may be possible to be a Christian without being part of a church, but it's not easy, because we need one another in all kinds of ways. We need the support of fellowship, worship and prayer; we need to belong and work together; we need to be part of a family, united in a common cause and sharing the same faith.

As Jesus said to his disciples, 'Where two or three are gathered in my name, I am there among them' (Matthew 18:20), and so Paul wrote to the Colossians, among others, telling them how much he longed to see them 'united in love' (Colossians 2:2).

On our own, we are but a shadow of what we could and ought to be. When we are joined together, in touch, linked by the love of Christ, then we become what God intends us to be: truly his people, his Church.

67 Belonging together

Reading Acts 2:38-47

Aim To emphasise that, as Christians, we are not designed to live in isolation but belong together.

Preparation In large bold letters print the following words:

SALT, JERRY, FISH, BUTTER, STRAWBERRIES, SULLIVAN, CHALK, SPADE, KNIFE, BRUSH, BAT, SAUCER, NEEDLE, BACON, STARS, JUDY, DR JEKYLL, IVY, HANSEL, ASHES

Print an ampersand sign (&) 20 times. Arrange the signs and words on a whiteboard, as follows:

SALT	&	
	&	JERRY
FISH	&	
	&	BUTTER
STRAWBERRIES	&	
	&	SULLIVAN
CHALK	&	
	&	SPADE
KNIFE	&	
	&	BRUSH
BAT	&	
	&	SAUCER
NEEDLE	&	
	&	BACON
STARS	&	
	&	JUDY
DR JEKYLL	&	
	&	IVY
HANSEL	&	
	&	ASHES

Print the following and retain for use during the talk:

PEPPER, TOM, CHIPS, BREAD, CREAM, GILBERT, CHEESE, BUCKET, FORK, DUSTPAN, BALL, CUP, THREAD, EGGS, STRIPES, PUNCH, MR HYDE, HOLLY, GRETEL, SACKCLOTH

If preferred, you may want to draw pictorial clues, rather than use words. Many of the items listed can be found in computer clip-art packages, should you choose this option. If you use pictures, you may find it effective to display the missing 'item' of each pair somewhere around the church, so that one of the young people can find it and bring it to you.

Talk

Tell the congregation that you are thinking today about matching pairs. Run through the list of names on the board, and then go through this again more slowly, asking if anyone can identify the missing word.

Each of these pairs belong together. When we think of one, we automatically think of the other, the two of them indissolubly linked in our minds. So much is this so that one seems incomplete without the other.

It is the same idea behind our reading from Acts. 'All who believed were together . . . day by day, as they spent much time together' (2:44, 46). In other words, says Luke, Christians belong together. We need each other if something vital isn't to be missing from our lives, both as individuals and as a church.

68   Ambassadors for Christ

Reading   2 Corinthians 5:11-21

Aim   To illustrate that as Christians we are called to be representatives of Christ, so that everything we do and stand for points to him.

Preparation   In large bold letters, print the following and arrange them in a column on a whiteboard:

RSPB, RNLI, RSPCA, EU, MBE, BSI, NSPCC, OBE, VC, NT, UNICEF, NHS, OHMS

Then display 10-12 colour pictures of national flags (A4-size or larger) on a second board or on the back of the first. Select flags that will be fairly easily recognised – for example, Australia, Brazil, Canada, China, Sweden, France, USA.

Talk   Hold up each flag and ask if anyone can identify which country it represents. At an international sporting occasion, such as the Olympic games, the flag of the winning athletes will be raised after each event, as a symbol that the competitors are representing their country. They do not only take part for themselves but on behalf of a nation, carrying their people's hopes with them.

Here is part of what Paul was talking about in the second of his letters to the Corinthians, and it is part equally of what it means to be the Church. We are ambassadors for Christ, called to live in such a way that we fly the flag for his kingdom, our lives lived not for our own glory but for his.

We can look at that in a slightly different way (display the list of abbreviations). Ask if anyone can tell you what each abbreviation stands for.

RSPB	Royal Society for the Protection of Birds
RNLI	Royal National Lifeboat Institution
RSPCA	Royal Society for the Prevention of Cruelty to Animals
EU	European Union
MBE	Member of the British Empire
BSI	British Standards Institution
NSPCC	National Society for the Prevention of Cruelty to Children
OBE	Order of the British Empire
VC	Victoria Cross
NT	National Trust

UNICEF   United Nations Children's Fund
NHS   National Health Service
OHMS   On Her Majesty's Service

All of these abbreviations stand for something, but, equally important, the organisations or awards that they represent stand in turn for
something themselves. The RSPB, RSPCA and NSPCC all stand for
prevention of cruelty. The National Trust stands for the protection
of our countryside. The NHS, RNLI and UNICEF stand, in different
ways, for the saving of human lives. The EU stands for economic
and social cooperation. The MBE, OBE and VC stand for achievement, courage or service. The British Standards Institution stands
for the maintaining of quality standards, and OHMS stands for
royal (or, in reality, government) authority or approval. In other
words, we are talking here about organisations committed to a
cause, or awards that speak of such commitment.

That, too, is what it means to be part of the Church, what is involved in
serving Christ. We are not Christians in name only but are called to work
for Christ's kingdom, committed to his service, furthering his purpose. Is
that true of us? What do we stand for? Whom do we represent?

MUSIC/SONGS OF PRAISE SERVICE

69   Make music in your hearts

Readings   Psalm 98; Colossians 3:16-17

Aim   To affirm the place of music and song in worship.

Preparation   On separate strips of card/paper, print the following in large bold letters:

> MUSICAL INSTRUMENT, MUSICAL CHAIRS, SONGS OF PRAISE, GOING FOR A SONG, MUSIC SYSTEM, FOLKSONG, MUSIC FESTIVAL, SONG THRUSH, THEME MUSIC, PLAINSONG, MUSICAL BOX, ROCK MUSIC, THE SOUND OF MUSIC, MUSICIAN, ORGAN MUSIC, EVENSONG, WATER MUSIC, SWAN SONG, ANNIE'S SONG, EUROVISION SONG CONTEST, SING A SONG OF SIXPENCE

Fix blutack to the back of each, ready for use later in the talk. Print the same words again and arrange on a board as follows:

```
    R O C K   M U S I C
          O R G A N   M U S I C
          F O L K S O N G
    M U S I C   F E S T I V A L
                  M U S I C A L       C H A I R S
        T H E   S O U N D   O F   M U S I C
            E V E N S O N G
            P L A I N S O N G
          M U S I C A L     I N S T R U M E N T
          M U S I C I A N
  S I N G   A   S O N G   O F   S I X P E N C E
      M U S I C   S Y S T E M
    E U R O V I S I O N   S O N G   C O N T E S T
              M U S I C A L   B O X
      G O I N G   F O R   A   S O N G
                T H E M E   M U S I C
          A N N I E S   S O N G
              S W A N   S O N G
        W A T E R   M U S I C
        S O N G   T H R U S H
        S O N G S   O F   P R A I S E
```

Turn this side of the board away from the congregation, to be revealed at the end of the talk, and use the other side for the quiz as below.

Talk   Tell the congregation that in keeping with a music and songs of praise service, you have prepared a quiz for them on a musical theme. All the answers have the word 'music' or 'song', or variants of these, in them. Read out the clues below, one by one, and as the correct answer is given stick it on to the board, arranging them as displayed on the next page:

- We make music on this: *Musical instrument*
- A traditional, boisterous and well-loved party game: *Musical chairs*
- The name of a long-running religious TV programme: *Songs of Praise*
- Being sold cheap, or the name of a once-popular TV programme on antiques: *Going for a Song*
- Another name for a hi-fi: *Music system*
- Another name for a traditional country song: *Folksong*
- A major event, held annually in such places as Cheltenham: *Music Festival*
- Like the blackbird and nightingale, this bird is celebrated for its song: *Song thrush*
- Music used at the start and end of a films and TV programmes: *Theme music*
- The name given to the chanting of monks: *Plainsong*
- A child's plaything: *Musical box*
- Heavy metal is an example of this: *Rock music*
- A film shown just about every Christmas! *The Sound of Music*
- The name we give to anyone who makes music: *Musician*
- The sort of music most often associated with church: *Organ music*
- A traditional church service in which the choir play a key role: *Evensong*
- A famous work by Handel that we might sing in the bath! *Water Music*
- The last performance of a celebrity: *Swan song*
- A John Denver song later played by the flautist James Galway: *Annie's Song*
- An international song competition held each year: *Eurovision Song Contest*
- The nursery rhyme that ends with a blackbird pecking off a nose: *Sing a Song of Sixpence*

MUSICAL   INSTRUMENT

MUSICAL   CHAIRS

SONGS   OF   PRAISE

GOING   FOR   A   SONG

MUSIC   SYSTEM

FOLKSONG

MUSIC   FESTIVAL

SONG   THRUSH

THEME   MUSIC

PLAINSONG

MUSICAL   BOX

ROCK   MUSIC

THE   SOUND   OF   MUSIC

MUSICIAN

ORGAN   MUSIC

EVENSONG

WATER   MUSIC

SWAN   SONG

ANNIES   SONG

EUROVISION   SONG   CONTEST

SING   A   SONG   OF   SIXPENCE

We can express ourselves through music in innumerable ways, just as there are an incalculable number of hymns, songs, melodies and tunes that we could have sung, played or listened to during this service. But we are not here simply to enjoy a good sing or tune, pleasurable enough though that might be. We are here for a reason: a reason that the various answers we've given tonight make clear.

Ask if anyone can see the first message hidden in the answers, and then read this through again yourself. 'Sing to the Lord a new song': that's why we're here, the motivation behind our songs and music today. That's why the hymns, songs and choruses we've shared were written, each designed to be offered to God in worship.

Turn over the board and reveal the second arrangement of words, and again ask if anyone can see the hidden message. 'Make music in your hearts': that's the second important ingredient of this service. We're not simply going through the motions, or at least we shouldn't be. What we sing should be offered from the heart; the music we make should be an expression of praise offered in thanksgiving and adoration. God has given us the gift of music, and we thank him *for* it; but, equally important, we thank him *through* it.

70   Sing to the Lord a new song

Readings

Psalm 96:1-9; Ephesians 5:15-20

Aim

To emphasise the importance of joyfully, spontaneously and faithfully giving praise and worship to God.

Preparation

Borrow CD recordings of recent chart hits from young people in your church, family or circle of friends, ensuring, if possible, that these are the most recent releases of each artist. Have these ready in the service to play a brief excerpt from each.

Talk

Ask how many of the young people like music. Who is their favourite group or singer and what is their favourite song? Tell the congregation that you have a pop quiz for them: all they have to do is listen to the snatches of music you are going to play and identify the name of the artist and song, and, if possible, give some idea of when the song was first released and what position it made in the charts. Play snippets from the CDs.

Some of you may harbour secret dreams of one day being pop stars, but few people have what it takes to make it to the top. Yet there is one sense in which we are all called not only to sing, but also, like the artists we've heard today, to constantly bring out new songs – and that sense is spelt out for us in the opening words of Psalm 96: 'O sing to the Lord a new song; sing to the Lord, all the earth. Sing to the Lord, bless his name; tell of his salvation from day to day' (vv. 1-2). Each one of us is called to offer worship to God, joyfully and sincerely to sing his praise; not as a duty but as a privilege, not as an obligation but as something we simply cannot help but do. Whether it is a hymn of praise or simply our hearts singing within us does not matter; what counts is that we want to respond in adoration and glad thanksgiving to the one who alone is worthy of all glory and honour, praise and worship.

ORDINARY SUNDAYS

71   Who do you say that I am?

Reading   Luke 9:21-27

Aim   To emphasise that we all need to make up our minds concerning who we believe Jesus to be and what he means for our lives.

Preparation   No special preparation is needed for this talk.

Talk   Ask if anyone in the congregation, young or old, has a nickname. Invite people to share what theirs is and why they are called it. Move from this to the following quiz, asking if anyone can tell you who is or was known by the following nicknames:

Lady of the Lamp	*Florence Nightingale*
The Iron Lady	*Margaret Thatcher*
Good Queen Bess	*Elizabeth I*
Hammer of the Scots	*Edward I*
Beefy	*Ian Botham*
Mr Fix-It	*Jimmy Saville*
The Bard	*William Shakespeare*
The Lionheart	*Richard I*
The King	*Elvis Presley*
The Great White Shark	*Greg Norman*
Old Blue Eyes	*Frank Sinatra*
The Desert Fox	*Rommel*
The Bulldog	*Winston Churchill*
The Welsh Wizard	*Lloyd George*
The Iron Duke	*Arthur Wellesley, Duke of Wellington*
The Black Pearl	*Pelé (Edson Arantes do Nascimento)*
The Longfellow	*Lester Piggott*
The Blonde Bombshell	*Marilyn Monroe (Norma Jean Mortenson)*
Posh Spice	*Victoria (Adams) Beckham*

All of these nicknames have one thing in common: they say something about the person they refer to, pointing to some aspect of their character or their achievements. So how about Jesus – what name was he known by? The answer may be a surprise, simply because it's so familiar: 'Christ' – not a second name or surname, but a title, almost a nickname, originally used only by his followers. Some also called him other names – Son of Man, Son of David, even the Son of God – but Christ is the one that has stuck, and it has done so for an important reason. Ask if anyone knows what it means. It translates as Messiah, Lord or Saviour, and, as such, to use it means to accept that Jesus is the one sent by God to redeem his people, to set us free, to establish God's kingdom here on earth.

So far as we know, the first person to use it in that way – effectively, as a name for Jesus – was Simon Peter. '[W]hat about you?' Jesus asked his disciples. 'Who do you say I am?' Peter answered, 'The Christ of God' (Luke 9:20, *NIV*). Here was Peter's way of saying who he believed Jesus to be, and in so doing he was professing his loyalty and commitment, expressing both faith and allegiance. That's why we speak of 'Jesus Christ'. The expression has become so familiar that we use it today without even thinking, but it's not just a name: it remains a declaration of commitment. Before we say it we need to ask ourselves: Who do *we* say Jesus is? Have we accepted him as Lord and Saviour in our lives?

72   Seeing things differently

Reading   Matthew 13:1-17

Aim   To illustrate that we have to look sometimes beneath surface appearances to catch a glimpse of spiritual realities.

Preparation   Copy and enlarge the following pictures, or draw your own if you prefer. (Larger versions of the pictures given here may be found in the Photocopy Masters section on pages 313-315.)

LOOK

LOOK BEFORE YOU LEAP

SIGHT

SIGHT

SIGHT

SIGHT

FORESIGHT

ꓘOOꓶ

LOOK THE OTHER WAY

C I 2 I

SEE EYE TO EYE

ALL EYES

EYE BALL

THE EYE OF THE STORM

GOOD-LOOKING

DOUBLE VISION

EYE SHADOW

I 4 I

AN EYE FOR AN EYE

X I'D

CROSS-EYED

Talk   Tell the congregation that you have some 'Catchphrase'-type clues to show them, each pointing to an expression concerned with sight or the way we see things. Hold up each picture in turn and ask if anyone can guess the phrase you have in mind.

The pictures together point us to another expression we often use: seeing something in a different light. In other words, sometimes we need to look beyond appearances if we are to glimpse the deeper truth beneath. That's what we had to do with each of the illustrations, it's what we often have to do in life generally, and it's what we have to do equally when it comes to things of God, as Jesus made clear in response to a question from his disciples concerning parables. The stories he told, like the Good Samaritan, the Lost Sheep, the Prodigal Son, the Mustard Seed and so on, can be understood in two ways: either as a simple story or as a personal challenge calling for an individual response. It all depends on the listener and on his or her openness to God. The same is true in innumerable other ways: one person may see the sky at night as declaring the wonder of God; another might see it as simply expressing the insignificance of humankind in terms of the vastness of the universe. One might interpret an event as God speaking to them, another as mere chance. Faith opens our eyes to a new dimension of life, a fresh perspective, seeing things differently. As Jesus put it, 'Blessed are your eyes, for they see, and your ears, for they hear' (Matthew 13:16). Or as Paul expressed it, in somewhat contrasting terms, 'We look not at what can be seen but at what cannot be seen; for what can be seen is temporary, but what cannot be seen is eternal' (2 Corinthians 4:18). Are our eyes open to what God is doing among us, the way he is working in our lives? Do we have eyes to see and ears to hear?

73   Foundations

Reading   Matthew 7:24-27

Aim   To stress the importance of basing our lives on something that will not let us down in times of testing or difficulty, and to emphasise that faith in Christ provides such a firm foundation.

Preparation   For this talk you need to have the game Kerplunk® (or, alternatively, the game Jenga®). The aim of this game is to pull out supporting sticks without causing a marble, or marbles, to drop down into your tray. (Similarly, in Jenga® it is to move a segment of wood without causing the tower to collapse.)

Talk   Invite four volunteers to come forward and play the game Kerplunk® (or Jenga®). (Carefully supervise the game to ensure it is played fairly, giving a gentle commentary of proceedings as you do so.) It doesn't take much to bring the marbles crashing down; each time a stick is removed the 'foundations' become a little less secure until eventually collapse is inevitable.

The lesson from this game is very simple, and, of course, it's the same message that Jesus was looking to get across in his parable of the wise and foolish builders. On what do we base our lives? What things do we count most important? What do we give our time and attention to? We may yearn after this and that, we may relentlessly pursue fame and fortune, we may hanker after possessions, but will such things bring us happiness? Will they be able to sustain us in times of crisis?

We could lose much in life without really being worse off, for though they may seem important so many things are ultimately trivial, as much a burden as a blessing. What we cannot afford to lose is a sense of meaning and purpose, a source of help in the present and hope for the future – in other words, a spiritual basis upon which all else rests. That is what God offers us in Christ: the assurance of his daily presence; an experience of life now in all its fullness and an assurance of life for all eternity; a sharing in his kingdom and an opportunity to help bring it to fruition. Listen to Christ's words, respond to his teaching, offer him our commitment and nothing in life or death will ever be able to shake our foundations.

74   From small beginnings

Readings   Matthew 13:31-32; Luke 17:5-6

Aim   To illustrate that God can use even a little faith to achieve great things.

Preparation   On separate sheets of card/paper, print the following in large bold letters and arrange as shown on a whiteboard. Use magnetic tape or blutack, so that the words can be reordered during the talk.

MIDDLEWEIGHT
FEATHERWEIGHT
SUPERHEAVYWEIGHT
LIGHTWEIGHT
FLYWEIGHT
HEAVYWEIGHT
WELTERWEIGHT
BANTAMWEIGHT

BELLOW
SPEAK
SCREAM
WHISPER
SHOUT
MURMUR

FLAME
BLAZE
INFERNO
FLICKER
SPARK
FIRE

BECK
SEA
STREAM
ESTUARY
SPRING
RIVER

STORM
HURRICANE
BREEZE
DRAUGHT
WIND
GALE

CROWD
GROUP
NATION
INDIVIDUAL
WORLD
PAIR

Talk   Show the congregation the words displayed on your whiteboard; then, run through the sequences, asking volunteers to place them in ascending order – that is, from the smallest to the largest. The amended sequences should run as follows:

FLYWEIGHT
FEATHERWEIGHT
LIGHTWEIGHT
BANTAMWEIGHT
WELTERWEIGHT
MIDDLEWEIGHT
HEAVYWEIGHT
SUPERHEAVYWEIGHT

WHISPER
MURMUR
SPEAK
SHOUT
BELLOW
SCREAM

SPARK
FLICKER
FLAME
FIRE
BLAZE
INFERNO

SPRING
BECK
STREAM
RIVER
ESTUARY
SEA

DRAUGHT
BREEZE
WIND
GALE
STORM
HURRICANE

INDIVIDUAL
PAIR
GROUP
CROWD
NATION
WORLD

Each sequence reminds us how something originally very small can swiftly grow into something very large. An insignificant whisper can develop into an ear-piercing scream; a tiny spring on a mountainside can become a mighty river; a chance spark can lead to a raging inferno; a draught of air can spiral into a powerful hurricane; and, albeit unlikely, a flyweight boxer or wrestler could, in time, develop into a superheavyweight. Minute beginnings can lead to disproportionately huge endings.

That's what Jesus was saying to his disciples in our two readings. We may not see much in the way of signs of his kingdom around us, and we may feel that there is little we can do to bring its coming closer, but that is to think in human terms rather than with God's understanding. A word here, an act there, can have effects far beyond anything we might imagine possible. God is able to work through the small and apparently insignificant to transform people and situations the world over, slowly but surely bringing his kingdom to fruition.

Never underestimate what God can do in your life. Never undervalue the way he can use you. Never underrate what your life and witness can achieve in his service. It may not seem much to you, but with God, when we offer it in faith, it is enough and more than enough.

75   A change of name

Readings   Acts 11:19-26; 1 Peter 2:9-10

Aim   To emphasise that being a Christian involves a change of identity in the sense of life taking on a new direction and purpose.

Preparation   On strips of paper/card, print the following in large bold letters and arrange down the left side of a whiteboard, as follows:

John
Bill
Mark
June
Jody
Cora
Kath
Tara
Beth
Millie

Similarly, print the following, arranging them down the centre of a whiteboard, as follows:

Alan
Mike
Phil
Andy
Polly
Cindy
Grace
Caleb

Finally, print the following and retain for display later in the service.

Joan
Jill
Mary
Jane
Judy
Lora
Kate
Zara

Seth
Billie
Jean/Alec/Aled/Sean
Luke/Mick
Gail/Paul
Anne/Judy
Sally/Billy
Sandy
Grant
Calum

Talk   Tell the congregation that you are thinking in this talk about names. Run through the first list of names; ask if anyone can make another name out of each simply by changing one letter. There are probably several alternatives, but a selection is given below:

John	*Joan*
Bill	*Jill*
Mark	*Mary*
June	*Jane*
Jody	*Judy*
Cora	*Lora*
Kath	*Kate*
Tara	*Zara*
Beth	*Seth*
Millie	*Billie*

Turning to the second list of names, ask if anyone can do something a little harder and make a new name by changing two letters.

Alan	*Jean/Alec/Aled/Sean*
Mike	*Luke/Mick*
Phil	*Gail/Paul*
Andy	*Anne/Judy*
Polly	*Sally/Billy*
Cindy	*Sandy*
Grace	*Grant*
Caleb	*Calum*

These are just some of the many names that can be changed from one to another, but, of course, there is no reason why most of us would want to change our name. Some people, though, do give

themselves different names. Ask if anyone can identify who the
following called themselves:

Mary Ann Evans	*George Eliot*
Currer, Ellis and Acton Bell	*Charlotte, Emily and Anne Brontë*
Priscilla White	*Cilla Black*
Harry Webb	*Cliff Richard*

How about the following cities – what were they once called?

Istanbul	*Constantinople*
Volgograd	*Stalingrad*
Beijing	*Peking*

And similarly, what were the following countries once called:

Zimbabwe	*Rhodesia*
Iran	*Persia*
Sri Lanka	*Ceylon*
Thailand	*Siam*
Zaire	*Belgian Congo*

Why were these various names changed? The reason, of course, was
to mark some kind of change of identity, whether of an individual
suddenly catapulted to fame, a country gaining independence, a town
throwing off its past, or an author seeking an unbiased response.

We see something similar to that in the Bible, associated with
people responding to the call of God: Abram is renamed Abraham
and his wife Sarai becomes Sarah; Jacob is given the name Israel;
Simon becomes Cephas, or Peter; and, of course, Saul becomes
Paul. In similar fashion, the followers of Jesus were given a nickname summing up their new allegiance and way of life: the familiar
term 'Christians'. We tend to use it today unthinkingly as nothing
more than a label, but it speaks, or should speak, of much more
than that. Its meaning is perhaps nowhere better summed up than
in the first letter of Peter: 'You are a chosen race, a royal priesthood,
a holy nation, God's own people, in order that you may proclaim the
mighty acts of him who called you out of darkness into his marvellous light. Once you were not a people but now you are God's
people; once you had not received mercy, but now you have
received mercy' (2:9-10).

That's what it means to be a Christian: to have one's life turned
around, given new meaning and a new direction, dying to self and
living for Christ. Is that what it means to you? Have you understood
what it means to bear the name of Christ?

76   Who created whom?

Readings   Psalm 139:13-18; Isaiah 49:1-6

Aim   To acknowledge and celebrate the fact that God created us.

Preparation   No special preparation is needed for this talk.

Talk   Tell the congregation that you have a quiz for them based on the characters created by particular authors. Ask if anyone can identify the creators of the following:

Maigret	*George Simenon*
Lord Peter Wimsey	*Dorothy L. Sayers*
Sherlock Holmes	*Sir Arthur Conan Doyle*
Peter Rabbit	*Beatrix Potter*
Inspector Morse	*Colin Dexter*
Hercule Poirot	*Agatha Christie*
Babe	*Dick King-Smith*
James Bond	*Ian Fleming*
Scarlett O'Hara	*Margaret Mitchell*
Mowgli	*Rudyard Kipling*
Captain Hook	*J. M. Barrie*
Dr Jekyll	*Robert Louis Stevenson*
Richard Hannay	*John Buchan*
The BFG	*Roald Dahl*
Jeeves	*P. G. Wodehouse*
Alice in Wonderland	*Lewis Carroll*
Tom Sawyer	*Mark Twain*
Christopher Robin	*A. A. Milne*
Heathcliff	*Emily Brontë*
Tess Durbeyfield	*Thomas Hardy*

These are all well-known characters, but none actually existed in their own right, each being the creation of different authors. Until recent years, apart from the natural act of childbirth this has been the closest we can get to creating anyone.

Today things are slightly different. Advances in genetics mean that scientists are able to clone human tissue or even engineer life in a test tube, but even so this is dependent upon the use of existing DNA and fraught with all kinds of practical and moral questions that leave many deeply troubled. The only one able to create life out of nothing is God. So we read in Psalm 139: 'It was you who formed my inward parts; you knit me together in my mother's womb. I praise you, for I am fearfully and wonderfully made. Your eyes beheld my unformed substance. In your book were written all the days that were formed for me, when none of them as yet existed' (vv. 13-14a, 16).

There is no denying that humankind can achieve much today, our knowledge and skills increasing year upon year, but we need to remember that those very skills and that ability to acquire and apply knowledge come from God, the one who alone created us and created all.

77　A matching picture

Reading

Matthew 5:13-16, 43-48

Aim

To stress how important it is for our deeds to measure up to our words, so that our lives themselves proclaim the gospel.

Preparation

From newspapers or magazines, find a selection of illustrated stories and cut out a selection of headlines/titles and corresponding pictures (one picture per story). Ensure that the picture very clearly relates to the headline/title, and keep a record of which picture fits which headline. You may wish to enlarge the pictures so that everyone in the congregation can see them clearly during the talk. Stick the pictures in prominent positions around the church prior to the service.

Talk

Tell the congregation that you have a selection of newspaper headlines/story titles, and explain that a picture matching each story is hidden somewhere in the church. Read out each headline/title in turn seeing who can be the first to identify the correct picture. For added effect, you may wish to display the headlines and matching pictures in a collage at the front of the church, building this up as each answer is given.

After you have finished, ask how difficult it was to match the pictures to the headlines/titles. The answer is (or at least should be!) that it was easy, in each case the two clearly belonging together.

So it should be with us. What we do should match what we say. What we are should correspond to what we claim to be. Of course, none of us is perfect, and there is no way that our lives will ever match that of Christ or even begin to, but that doesn't mean we shouldn't seek to become as much like him as possible. If our words bear no relation to our deeds, and the way we live is contrary to the faith we proclaim, then few people will take our faith seriously. Worse than that, many will be put off, deciding that if we're any advertisement for the Christian faith, then they don't want to know.

'Let your light shine before others, so that they may see the good deeds you do and give glory to your Father in heaven' (Matthew 5:16, own translation). Do people see any light in us? Do they glimpse something of the Christ we claim to serve? How far do we give a matching picture to others?

78   Breaking down the barriers

Readings   Ephesians 2:13-18; Colossians 2:13-15; 3:5-11

Aim   To offer a reminder that God in Christ has broken down the barriers that separate us from him.

Preparation   This talk requires a fair amount of work but the visual impact, and the way this simply but effectively communicates the message, make it more than worth it. You will need 54 blank one-inch-square cubes. The best way to make these is by sawing up a length of one-by-one timber. You will need to use a T-Box to ensure that each cube is perfectly square, otherwise the talk will end in disaster! Using a black marker pen, write a letter on each of the bricks so that they can be assembled into a wall as set out below.

(You could make the cubes out of card, but it will be difficult, if not impossible, this way to ensure uniform construction, which may mean that the wall below, or the cross-shape used later in the talk, comes tumbling down halfway through. Another alternative, and perhaps the simplest, is to use children's alphabet building blocks, if you can get hold of them. If you use this method, prepare the cross-shape before the talk, and discard the bricks from the word-search wall as each word is identified.)

J	E	A	L	O	U	S	Y	H
E	D	E	E	R	G	S	S	A
N	D	O	U	B	T	I	E	T
V	E	D	I	R	P	N	I	R
Y	M	A	L	I	C	E	L	E
S	S	E	N	N	A	E	M	D

Disassemble the wall, brick by brick, starting from the left-hand side and working across from left to right in each row. As you remove each brick, write another letter on the back, as follows: on J write Y, on E: T, on A: I, on L: L, on O: I; on U: T, on S: S, on Y: O, on H: H, on E: F, on D: O, on E: L, on E: L, on R: A, on G: W, on S: G, on S: N, on A: I, on N: D, on D: I, on O: V, on U: I, on B: D, on T: E, on I: H, on E: T, on T: N, on V: W, on E: O, on D: D, on I: N, on R: E, on P: K, on N: O, on I: R, on R: B, on Y: S, on M: A, on A: H, on L: E, on I: H, on C: T, on E: S, on L: I, on E: R, on S: H, on S: C, on E: H, on N: G, on N: U, on A: O, on E: R, on M: H, on D: T.

Reassemble the wall in a prominent position at the front of the church. During the latter part of the talk you will need a nine-inch long, one-inch wide strip of wood, strong enough to bear the weight of wooden 'bricks' stacked across it.

Talk

Tell the congregation that you want to think today about the things that separate us from God, that prevent us from knowing him as fully as he would like, or living life as fully as he desires. In his letter to the Ephesians, the Apostle speaks of such things in terms of a dividing wall of hostility between us. Point to the wall you have assembled and explain that it contains a wordsearch, each of the words within it being something that separates us from both God and one another.

Starting with the top row, and working along each in turn, ask if anyone can spot a hidden word, reading either along or downwards. The words should be identified in the following order (if they are not, take them down and store them until the appropriate time):

JEALOUSY, HATRED, ENVY, GREED, SIN, LIES, DOUBT, PRIDE, MALICE, MEANNESS

As each word is identified, remove the bricks, reverse them, and, rearrange them into the shape of a cross as illustrated below, starting at the bottom left corner of the cross and ensuring that the letters are in the exact order shown and facing the congregation (note that you will need to place the wooden support centrally above the seventh row of bricks, to support the 'cross beams'). Continue until all the words in the word-search have been identified and you have successfully constructed the 'cross'.

			T	H	R			
			O	U	G			
H	C	H	R	I	S	T	H	E
H	A	S	B	R	O	K	E	N
D	O	W	N	T	H	E	D	I
			V	I	D			
			I	N	G			
			W	A	L			
			L	O	F			
			H	O	S			
			T	I	L			
			I	T	Y			

We have successfully demolished the wall that separates us from God. If only it were that simple in real life. The fact is that however hard we try we cannot demolish the wall through our own efforts, such things as greed, envy, hatred and pride holding us captive. Even if we can overcome them, we can never change sufficiently to put ourselves right with God. Yet demolishing the wall *is* as simple as we have seen and even more so, not through anything we've done but through what God has done for us in Jesus Christ.

Draw attention to the cross you have made. Ask the congregation, or a single volunteer, to read from the top of the cross downwards:

THROUGH CHRIST HE HAS BROKEN DOWN THE DIVIDING WALL OF HOSTILITY

What we cannot do, God has done for us, overcoming through his love in Christ what we can never hope to overcome ourselves. It needs us only to acknowledge our faults, confess what is wrong and seek his help; he has done the rest!

79   Eating together

Reading

Luke 22:14-23

Aim

This talk is designed for use in a service of Holy Communion, and aims to explore the meaning of the Lord's Supper as an occasion that emphasises the fellowship we share with Christ and with all his people.

Preparation

On separate strips of card, print the following in large bold letters:

RESTAURANT, MCDONALDS, PARTY, PICNIC, BANQUET, DINING ROOM, FEAST, RECEPTION, LUNCHEON, GARDEN PARTY, CAFE, CHIP SHOP, BUFFET, BARBECUE

Attach a small piece of blutack to each and set aside for use later in the talk. Print a second copy of each of the above, and arrange them on a whiteboard as follows:

```
        R E C E P T I O N
                  C H I P     S H O P
        B A N Q U E T
    M C D O N A L D S
    L U N C H E O N
            B A R B E C U E
        G A R D E N     P A R T Y
          R E S T A U R A N T
      F E A S T
            B U F F E T
            P A R T Y
            P I C N I C
      C A F E
    D I N I N G     R O O M
```

Retain the board for use later in the talk.

Print the following letters, ensuring that they are the same size as the words you printed earlier:

E, A, T, I, N, G, T, O, G, E, T, H, E, R

Arrange these on a second whiteboard, as on the next page:

E
A
T
I
N
G
T
O
G
E
T
H
E
R

Display this at the front of the church, ready to begin the talk.

Talk   Pointing to the second of the two whiteboards, tell the congregation that you want to think today about places and occasions when we eat together. Explain that you have prepared a simple quiz to help do that: all of the clues point to places where we might share a meal, or particular types of meals. As each answer is given, replace the appropriate letter with the correct word, as set out after the quiz questions below:

- There are many kinds of these: Chinese and Indian to name but two – *Restaurant*
- This is a popular place for hamburgers and milkshakes – *McDonald's*
- We may be invited to this on someone's birthday – *Party*
- A meal eaten out of doors, perhaps from a hamper– *Picnic*
- A particularly sumptuous and special feast – *Banquet*
- The place where people traditionally eat when at home – *Dining room*
- A meal held after a wedding or important occasion – *Reception*
- A posh word for the meal eaten in the middle of the day – *Luncheon*
- Outdoor meal associated with cucumber sandwiches – *Garden party*
- A downmarket sort of restaurant – *Cafe*
- A sumptuous meal that is also the name for an ice lolly – *Feast*
- A traditional British place for buying a takeaway meal – *Chip shop*
- A light self-service meal or the place to buy food on a train – *Buffet*

- A meal grilled and eaten outdoors – *Barbecue*

```
            R E S T A U R A N T
    M C D O N A L D S
        P A R T Y
      P I C N I C
          B A N Q U E T
    D I N I N G   R O O M
    R E C E P T I O N
  L U N C H E O N
              G A R D E N   P A R T Y
        C A F E
      F E A S T
  C H I P   S H O P
    B U F F E T
        B A R B E C U E
```

All these places and meals show what an important role eating together plays in our lives. It is first, of course, a way of satisfying our hunger, meeting our physical need for sustenance. It is often also a way of marking a special occasion through a luncheon, party, banquet or reception. Equally, and perhaps most important, it is a way of sharing fellowship as well as food, of building up friendships, getting to know people better and cementing relationships.

We haven't yet thought, though, of one more meal; a meal that we share together here in church and a meal that has something in common with all the things we've thought of above. (Display the first board you prepared earlier, and ask if anyone can spot the hidden message: THE LORD'S SUPPER.) This meal too satisfies our need: not our physical but our spiritual hunger. Those who hunger and thirst after righteousness will be filled, said Jesus, and we are reminded here of his promise to give us living bread. Here also we mark a special occasion: the last supper Jesus shared with his disciples before he faced the cross. At this table, together we remember his death but celebrate also his resurrection and look forward to his coming. Finally, through sharing here we share fellowship with Jesus and with all his people, the Church in every place and time. We grow closer to him and to one another, cementing the bond of love that unites us.

'He took a loaf of bread, and when he had given thanks, he broke it and gave it to them, saying, "This is my body, which is given for you. Do this in remembrance of me"' (Luke 22:19): the call of Christ to the simplest of meals, yet the most important time of eating together there can be!

80   Self-centred, God-centred?

Readings   Proverbs 16:18-19; Philippians 2:1-11

Aim   To ask whom we put at the centre of our lives: Christ or ourselves.

Preparation   Copy the pictures shown in the talk below (for larger versions, see Photocopy Masters section on pages 316-317). You may want to enlarge these further so that they can be clearly seen by all during the talk. Alternatively, you may wish to draw your own, using these as a guideline.

Talk   Tell the congregation that you have prepared a selection of 'Catch-phrase' clues; some pointing to single words and others to well-known proverbs. Ask who can identify what the following stand for (the answers are given beneath each clue)

SELF

SELF-CENTRED

CONCEITED IDIOT

PRIDE GOES BEFORE A FALL

₂4 1, 1, 1, BOOTS

TOO BIG FOR ONE'S BOOTS

1 LOOKING

LOOKING AFTER NUMBER ONE

BIG-HEADED

BLOWING ONE'S OWN TRUMPET

These are all ways in which we might put ourselves first; puffed up perhaps with our own importance, or thinking only of our own comfort and well-being. What a contrast that is to the example of Jesus that Paul speaks of in his letter to the Philippians: 'Do nothing out of personal ambition,' he writes, 'but in humility, value others as much as yourselves, being concerned more about their well-being than your own' (Philippians 2:1-4, own translation).

What sort of people are we? Who takes pride of place in our lives? Is our chief aim to look after number one, or do we make time for others, ready to put them first where necessary? Are we puffed up with our own importance, or do we recognise our limitations and the gifts of others? Are we concerned with serving our own interests, pursuing our own ends, or do we seek, above all else, to discern the will of God and to further his purpose? In short, are we self-centred or God-centred?

81   The key to it all

Reading   John 14:1-7

Aim   To illustrate that Jesus alone can set us free from all that holds us captive.

Preparation   Borrow or buy a simple combination-padlock chain, such as is commonly used to secure a bicycle, with a four-number code, each between one and six. Print out the following text from John 14:6 on the centre of a piece of paper:

> Jesus said . . . I am the way, and the truth, and the life. No one comes to the Father except through me.

Fold this in half and then in half again, and place it in a padlockable box/container. Seal the box/container with the combination padlock. Make sure you do not forget the code, or the order in which the numbers go! Using brightly coloured pieces of card cut out four large key shapes: blue for the first, green for the second, red for the third and yellow for the last (in ascending alphabetical order, to avoid confusion). From the lists below, select one text for each of the code numbers. For example, if your code is 3653, choose one text from the third list, one from the sixth list, one from the fifth list and finally another from the third list.

LIST 1

Genesis 2:24: Therefore a man leaves his father and his mother and clings to his wife, and they become one flesh.

Matthew 26:40b: . . . he said to Peter, 'So, could you not stay awake with me one hour?'

Mark 8:14: Now the disciples had forgotten to bring any bread; and they had only one loaf with them in the boat.

Ephesians 4:4-5: There is one body and one Spirit, just as you were called to the one hope of your calling, one Lord, one faith, one baptism, one God and Father of all, who is above all and through all and in all.

LIST 2

Matthew 6:24a: No one can serve two masters . . .

Mark 6:7a: He called the twelve and began to send them out two by two.

Mark 12:42: A poor widow came and put in two small copper coins which are worth a penny.

Acts 28:30: He lived there for two whole years at his own expense and welcomed all who came to him.

LIST 3

Luke 11:5: Suppose you have a friend, and you go to him at midnight and say to him, 'Friend, lend me three loaves of bread.'

Acts 11:11: At that very moment three men, sent to me from Caesarea, arrived at the house where we were.

1 Corinthians 13:13: And now faith, hope, and love abide, these three; and the greatest of these is love.

Hebrews 11:23a: By faith Moses was hidden by his parents for three months after his birth.

LIST 4

Ezekiel 1:5a: In the middle of it was something like four living creatures.

Daniel 7:3a: . . . four great beasts came up out of the sea.

John 11:17: When Jesus arrived, he found that Lazarus had already been in the tomb for four days.

Acts 21:9: He had four unmarried daughters who had the gift of prophecy.

LIST 5

Matthew 25:2a: Five of them were foolish, and five were wise.

John 4:17b-18a: Jesus said to her, 'You are right in saying, "I have no husband"; for you have had five husbands.'

Luke 16:28a: I have five brothers.

John 5:2: Now in Jerusalem by the Sheep Gate there is a pool, called in Hebrew Bethzatha, which has five porticoes.

LIST 6

Ruth 3:15b: . . . he measured out six measures of barley.

1 Samuel 17:4: And there came out from the camp of the Philistines a champion named Goliath, of Gath, whose height was six cubits and a span.

Proverbs 6:16a: There are six things that the Lord hates.

Acts 11:12b: These six brothers also accompanied me, and we entered the man's house.

In bold marker pen, write the relevant Bible reference on the front of the appropriately coloured 'key' in large letters and numbers. Write out the full text on the back of the key. Using blutack, stick the four keys in semi-concealed positions around the church. Finally, on a piece of white card write the combination code as the combination numbers are 'discovered' during the service.

Talk   Tell the congregation that you have a very important document locked away in your box, but that you need their help in unlocking the padlock. Ask if anyone would like to have a go at cracking the combination code. Allow two volunteers up to a minute each on this. Provided you have thoroughly jumbled up the code numbers on the lock, the chances of them successfully discovering the code are infinitesimal. Now tell the congregation that you have some clues that should lead us to the numbers we need. Explain that there are four keys hidden around the church, each of which carries a passage of scripture referring to a number between one and six. Ask if someone can find and bring you a blue key. Invite the person who finds it to announce the text and read the passage (if necessary, repeat the passage yourself for the benefit of the hard of hearing). Ask the congregation what number is hidden in the message and write this on your blank sheet of card. Repeat this process for the green, red and yellow keys. Display the four numbers and then ask someone to apply the code and open the box.

We need to know the code if we are to get into the box. Without it, we would have to force our way in as best we could. Inside the box, however, we find another passage of scripture (unfold the sheet with the John 14:6 reference on it, and ask someone to read it for you). Jesus is talking here not about getting into something as ordinary and insignificant as a box, but about entering the kingdom of heaven, about discovering the way to life, and about gaining access to God the Father. How do we do that? Not through any secret knowledge or through any action on our part, and certainly not through forcing our way in, but through committing our lives to Christ and following him as best we are able. He is the one who unlocks the door to God and who opens the way to his kingdom: Jesus Christ – the way, the truth and the life.

82   A God not made with hands

Reading   Isaiah 46:1-10

Aim   To warn of the danger of creating God in our own image and forgetting that we are made in his.

Preparation   In large bold letters, print the following sets of words and display them on a whiteboard. Do not include the asterisks: these are simply for reference, indicating which is the odd one out in each group.

OIL	IRON
GAS	BRASS*
NUCLEAR POWER*	GOLD
COAL	SILVER
DIAMOND	GROWMORE*
RUBY	BONEMEAL
PEARL	MANURE
ZIRCONIUM*	COMPOST
SUNLIGHT	STREAM
STARLIGHT	CANAL*
MOONLIGHT	RIVER
CANDLELIGHT*	BROOK
WOOD	POND
LEATHER	RESERVOIR*
PLASTIC*	SEA
STONE	LAKE
NYLON*	GLACÉ CHERRY*
WOOL	AVOCADO PEAR
SILK	ORANGE
COTTON	KIWI FRUIT

Talk   Taking a group of words at a time, ask whether anyone in the congregation can identify which is the odd one out and why. All of the things listed are what we might term natural or God-given rather than man-made, except for the odd one out in each case. In all of these it's easy enough to spot the difference, but not everything can be so easily distinguished. Paradoxically, nowhere is that more so than when it comes to God. Without realising it, we can sometimes create him in our own likeness, limiting him to the way we think, expecting him to act in the way we want, closed to anything that might contradict our understanding or experience of life. More dangerous still, we can subconsciously worship things like money, power and possessions, our lives devoted to these despite our paying lip-service to God.

We need to remember that, in fact, *we* are created in *his* image, and any knowledge, skills or understanding we may have are a pale reflection of his infinite wisdom and power. Give thanks, yes, for everything human beings are able to achieve, celebrate everything God has given, but never forget that he made us, that we owe our all to him, and that he alone is worth serving.

83   Honest to God

Readings   Job 3:11, 20-21a; Psalm 66:16-20

Aim   To encourage honesty in prayer, recognising that since God knows what we really think there is no point hiding our true feelings and telling him what we believe he wants to hear.

Preparation   Ask between six and eight people to prepare four statements about themselves which they are willing to share in church, at least one of which must be false. (If just one statement is false, this should seem fairly credible; if two statements are false, one of these may be ludicrously outlandish.)

Talk   Ask the congregation how good they are at spotting when people are and aren't telling the truth. Tell them that you want to test their abilities, and explain that certain members of the congregation are going to divulge four things about themselves, some of which may be true and some of which may not be. Invite the people you have chosen to come forward, one at a time, and after each has spoken, run through each of the statements they made, asking for a show of hands as to whether people believed them or not. Then ask the individual in question to reveal which statements were true and which false. At the end, ask the congregation how they did in spotting the untruths.

Of course, the volunteers only told untruths because they were told to, but often in life there are other reasons. Sometimes we tell a white lie to protect someone or avoid hurting their feelings. Sometimes we deal in half-truths, leaving out details about something that we'd prefer no one else knew about. Sometimes again we simply lie to avoid being found out, desperately hoping to escape the consequences of our actions. We do all this not only with other people but also with God. There are some things that we are happy to tell God about ourselves, other things that we are not so happy about; some things we are ready and even proud to admit, others that we are ashamed of and try to hide. That is why the book of Psalms is so important because in it we see a collection of prayers in which the authors are completely, and sometimes shockingly, honest to God. There is no pretending in the psalms, no covering up the unpalatable and resorting to half-truths. There is no special language, a sticking to safe, spiritual, religious subjects. The psalm writers tell God how they are feeling; if they have done wrong they acknowledge it; if they are angry they vent that anger at God; if they are depressed they tell him how they feel; if they believe he's been unfair they tell him so; if he seems far away they pour out their feelings before him; if they are puzzled and confused by the apparent injustices of life they lay it on the line, telling God straight out.

> Why, O Lord, do you stand far off? Why do you hide yourself in times of trouble? (*Psalm 10:1*)

> My God, my God, why have you abandoned me? Why are you so far from helping me, from heeding my groans? I cry to you by day, O God, but you do not answer; and by night, but gain no respite. (*Psalm 22:1-2, own translation*)

> How long, O Lord? Will you forget me for ever? How long will you hide your face from me? How long must I bear pain in my soul and have sorrow in my heart all day long? How long shall my enemy be exalted over me? (*Psalm 13:1-2*)

> O God, why do you cast us off for ever? Why does your anger smoke against the sheep of your pasture? (*Psalm 74:1*)

> Rise up, O judge of the earth; give to the proud what they deserve! O Lord, how long shall the wicked, how long shall the wicked exult? (*Psalm 94:2-3*)

The language in the book of Job is even more blunt:

> Why did I not die at birth, expire when I was brought from my mother's womb? Why do those consumed by despair continue to see the light of day, and why is life given to the bitter in soul who long for death only for it not to come? (*Job 3:11, 20-21a, own translation*)

In each of these examples, there is no attempt to hide the writer's true feelings, no saying the right thing and bottling up what he actually wants to say. Here, surely, is what prayer should be about but so often isn't: being honest with God. Sadly, we tend to feel some things cannot be said to God, that he will be shocked if we express our true feelings. The writers of the Psalms and the book of Job thought differently. They understood that God knows the truth about us, and that he therefore want us to be honest with him so that he can respond in his own way to each situation. He may not do what we ask or give what we want, but when we are honest in prayer we can be sure that he will hear and respond. To use words from the Psalms once more:

> I cried aloud to him, and he was extolled with my tongue. If I had cherished iniquity in my heart, the Lord would not have listened. But truly God has listened; he has given heed to the words of my prayer. Blessed be God, because he has not rejected my prayer or removed his steadfast love from me. (*Psalm 66:17-20*)

84 Hearing God's call

Reading   1 Samuel 3:2-10

Aim   To illustrate the difficulties involved in discerning God's voice, but to emphasise that he *does* speak, through different people in different ways and at different times, and often in moments we least expect.

Preparation   Make a tape recording of various people talking, some from the radio or television and others from within your church fellowship. Ensure that there is a mixture of hard and easy voices, some that will be easy to identify and others that will be virtually impossible.

Talk   Play the tape of the voices you've recorded, asking after each one if anybody can identify the speaker. Sometimes we can tell easily who's speaking, at other times it's almost impossible to be sure. This might give us some insight into the story of Samuel as a boy in the temple. Suddenly he is conscious of a voice calling him, but who? His assumption is that it must be the priest Eli, and he assumes the same again the second and third times he hears the voice calling. Indeed, he may have carried on doing so ad infinitum if Eli hadn't recognised that it was God speaking, calling Samuel to respond.

Are we any better at recognising when God is speaking to us? I doubt it, for it's not easy to know. Few, if any, discern a recognisable voice, an unmistakable call. Instead God speaks in different ways; sometimes through others, sometimes through the words of scripture, sometimes through daily events, sometimes through conscience, or prayer, a sermon or worship, and so we could go on. We do not know *when* he will speak or *how*, but his call comes nonetheless, and he will go on calling until finally the penny drops and we respond. Are we ready to hear? Are we open to what he might say? Are we willing to respond?

85   A friend in need

Readings   Proverbs 17:17; 27:6, 10; John 15:12-17

Aim   To emphasise that Jesus counts us his friends, and that we can rely on him to be a friend in time of need, but also to ask whether we live faithfully as his friends in turn.

Preparation   In large bold letters, print and display the following riddle:

> My first's in DEFENDER and not in DENY,
> My second's in CARING as well as RELY,
> My third is in LOVING and seen in BELIEVE,
> My fourth's found in GIVE as well as RECEIVE,
> My fifth's in DEPENDING and not in DEFECT,
> My last's in ACCEPTED but not in REJECT.
> Now put these together, the answer will teach us
> Just what sort of person in Jesus we're given.

On separate slips of paper/card, print the following, and affix blutack to the back of each. Retain the slips for use later in the talk.

DEFENDS, CARES, BELIEVES, ACCEPTS, LOVING, DEPENDABLE, GIVES

Talk   Ask if anyone can solve the riddle. The answer, of course, is FRIEND. And the words of the riddle remind us of just some of the things involved in friendship. A friend is someone who defends us in time of need (place the word DEFENDS on the board), who cares about us (place the word CARES, aligning it as set out below), who believes in us and looks for the best (place the word BELIEVES), who accepts us as we are rather than for anything we might become (place the word ACCEPTS), who is loving towards us (place the word LOVING), who is dependable (place the word DEPENDABLE) and who gives freely in friendship (place the word GIVES).

```
    D E F E N D S
      C A R E S
    B E L I E V E S
    A C C E P T S
      L O V I N G
  D E P E N D A B L E
      G I V E S
```

Friends like that, of course, are hard to find but according to John there is one who offers such friendship to all. 'You are my friends,' says Jesus (John 15:14-15), 'if you do what I command you. I do not call you servants any longer, because the servant does not know what the master is doing; but I have called you friends, because I have made known to you everything that I have heard from my Father.' Here is the friendship that God offers us in Christ; a friend from whose love nothing can ever separate us; who not only stands with us in life but has also stood with us in death, believing in us so much he was willing to die for us; who accepts us as we are, loves and cares for us as no other, defends us from evil and gives us life in all its fullness – a friend on whom we can depend in time of need. That is the friend we have in Jesus. What sort of friend does he have in us?

86 No limits

Reading Philippians 4:10-14

Aim To emphasise that with God's help, we can achieve more than we might imagine possible.

Preparation No special preparation is needed for this talk.

Talk Begin by asking the congregation the following questions:

- What did Jan Zelezny throw 318 feet 10 inches? *Javelin*
- Who leapt an astonishing 60 feet 5 inches in the Triple Jump? *Jonathan Edwards*
- Who scored 375 runs in a test match, and for which team? *Brian Lara, West Indies*
- Who was sold to which football team for £35 million? *Luis Figo, Real Madrid*
- Which player has scored the highest break in professional snooker, and how many points did he score? *Tony Drago, scoring 149 points after a free ball was called*
- Who topped the European Order of Merit for five years in a row, and in which sport? *Colin Montgomerie, golf*
- Which woman won 167 singles matches and 165 doubles, and in which sport? *Martina Navratilova, tennis*
- Who set a world land-speed record of 633.468mph and in what car? *Richard Noble in Thrust 2*
- Who scored the most ever goals in the old First Division, and how many? *Dixie Deans scored 60*
- Who won the most majors in the world of golf, and how many? *Jack Nicklaus, 18*
- Which national Rugby Union team scored the most points in a World Cup, and how many did they score? *New Zealand scored 145 points against Japan*

All these are examples of those who have pushed back the limits of human achievement, accomplishing things that people previously had never imagined possible. How did they do it? By refusing to give in; by trying and trying again, convinced that the goals they had set themselves were possible despite what the doubters might say.

We see something similar to that in those words of Paul to the Philippians. Writing from a prison cell, having been arrested on account of his faith and having faced persecution and hostility throughout his ministry, he was yet able to say to the Philippians, 'I can do all things through him who strengthens me' (4:13). Despite all the limits people had attempted to place upon his ministry, all their efforts to frustrate and impede him, Paul knew that with God's help he could accomplish more than he could ever begin to ask or imagine. He knew that God was always helping him to push back the limits that little bit further. So it can be for us too. Never underestimate what God is able to do in your life. Never dismiss the way he is able to work through you. Never lose sight of his ability to work in ways exceeding all your expectations. In our own strength we may be able to do little, but with him by our side we are able to say, with Paul, 'I can do all things through him who strengthens me.'

87   That's the limit

Reading   1 Corinthians 8:1-13; 10:23-11:1

Aim   To illustrate that freedom in Christ nonetheless involves responsibilities that limit our behaviour.

Preparation   Copy and enlarge the following signs (larger versions may be found in the Photocopy Masters section on pages 318-319):

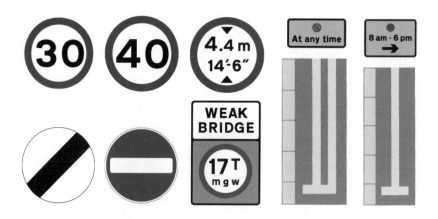

Talk   Hold up the various road signs, asking what they mean and where they might be found. The 30mph limit, for example, will be found on most town roads, with 40mph in certain cases. The national speed limit means 60mph on single-carriage roads and 70mph on dual carriageways and motorways. Such limits may sometimes be frustrating, especially if we are in a hurry or if there is no one and no traffic around, but they are designed for our own safety and that of those around us. Traffic signs are not the only limits imposed on us though. A plug or extension lead frequently carries the direction 'maximum load: 13 amps'; a cheque card or credit card often has a £100 ceiling placed on it; a lift has a certain number of people it is allowed to carry; and so we could continue. In daily life, various limits are imposed on us, each for a purpose. Imagine a world in which everyone could do as they pleased, a world in which there was no law and order, and nothing to keep the powerful or greedy in check. The result would be chaos.

As Christians, similarly, we have limits placed upon us. Although Jesus tells us that the truth will set us free, we need to exercise that freedom with restraint and sensitivity. Some actions are plainly wrong, and to indulge in them would effectively be to deny our faith. Others, though, may seem harmless, even right. 'Why shouldn't we do this?' we might ask. What's wrong with living like that? technically we may be right, but we need always to consider the feelings, circumstances, sensitivities and weaknesses of others. So it was that Paul urged caution on the Corinthians concerning the eating of food previously offered to idols. 'Take care', he writes (1 Corinthians 8:9; 10:23), 'that this liberty of yours does not somehow become a stumbling-block to the weak.' 'All things are lawful, but not all are beneficial.' In other words, think how your actions might be interpreted by others, consider whether what's right for you is necessarily right for others. No one can say what those things might be, for they depend upon particular situations, but we need to remember that as well as being responsible for ourselves, in some ways we are also responsible for others.

88   Raising a smile

Readings   Psalm 30; Luke 6:20-21

Aim   To emphasise that sorrow will not be allowed to have the last word, that God is always looking to bring us laughter and joy, whether in this life or the next.

Preparation   Copy and enlarge the following pictures, to be used as 'Catchphrase' clues during the talk. (Larger versions may be found in the Photocopy Masters section on pages 320-321).

Down in the mouth

As miserable as sin

Down in the dumps

Raising a smile

As happy as Larry

Talk   Tell the congregation that you have something today to cheer them up; some 'Catchphrase' clues on the subject of joy and sorrow. Display the pictures one by one, asking if anyone can identify the phrase you're looking for. We will all experience sorrow at some time or other, and some perhaps more than our fair share, for it is the price of happiness and part of being human. But though God permits sorrow, his desire is always to bring us joy, to bring a smile to our lips and a song to our hearts. As David put it in Psalm 30 (v. 5b), 'Weeping may linger for the night, but joy comes with the morning.' That is not to say that sorrow always passes overnight, but that joy will ultimately return in God's own time. So Jesus told the disciples, speaking of the final fulfilment of God's purpose, 'Blessed are you who weep now, for you will laugh.'

We cannot afford to be blasé about suffering or sorrow, glossing over these or making out they are any less real than they in fact are, but as Christians we have the assurance that tears and sadness will not have the last word; that joy and laughter will return, by God's grace.

89   A question of faith

Readings   Proverbs 2:1-15; Matthew 7:7-8

Aim   To emphasise that God is happy for us to ask questions concerning our faith, and that faith itself asks questions of us.

Preparation   Print the following in large bold letters and display on a whiteboard:

> _____ can a man be born again?
>
> _____ more shall I say?
>
> _____ is he born king of the Jews?
>
> _____ will these things happen?
>
> _____ must I do to inherit eternal life?
>
> _____ can we know the way?
>
> _____ do you look for the living among the dead?
>
> _____ is your faith?
>
> _____ can we sing the Lord's song?
>
> _____ do you stand there looking into heaven?
>
> _____ is this man?
>
> _____ shall these things be?
>
> _____ do you say that I am?
>
> _____ is your God?
>
> _____ of these three was a neighbour?

Next, on individual pieces of card, print the following words in large bold letters, in each case making the number specified. Attach a piece of blutack to the back of them, and retain for use during the service.

> WHAT (2)
>
> WHO (2)
>
> WHEN (1)
>
> WHERE (3)
>
> WHY (2)
>
> HOW (4)
>
> WHICH (1)

Talk   Ask the congregation what the words 'what', 'who', 'when', 'where', 'why', 'how' and 'which' have in common. The answer, of course, is that they are all used in asking questions. They also have another thing in common, something that may come as a surprise, for each one is found many times in the Bible. Turn to the display on your whiteboard, and ask if anyone can suggest the missing word from these biblical verses. As they do so, stick the word on to the board, as follows:

HOW can a man be born again?

WHAT more shall I say?

WHERE is he born king of the Jews?

WHEN will these things happen?

WHAT must I do to inherit eternal life?

HOW can we know the way?

WHY do you look for the living among the dead?

WHERE is your faith?

HOW can we sing the Lord's song?

WHY do you stand there looking into heaven?

WHO is this man?

HOW shall these things be?

WHO do you say that I am?

WHERE is your God?

WHICH of these three was a neighbour?

These are just some of the many questions within the Bible; questions that people asked centuries ago. Ours may be different, but many still ask questions today as they seek for understanding. Some look for answers before feeling able to come to faith, others seek understanding to help them grow and mature as Christians. What's important is that they feel able to ask, just as those who first posed the questions felt able to, confident that God would answer. As the book of Proverbs puts it, 'If you cry out for insight, and raise your voice for understanding, if you seek for it as for hidden treasures – then you will understand the fear of the Lord and find the knowledge of God. For the Lord gives wisdom; from his mouth come knowledge and understanding' (Proverbs 2:3-6, own translation).

We're not, though, talking here simply about questions *we* might ask, but also questions that might be asked *of us*. 'Which of these three was a neighbour?' asked Jesus, after telling the parable of the Good Samaritan. 'What about you? Who do you say that I am?' he asked the disciples. 'Where is your faith?' These are questions asked not only then but also now; questions for us today. The Bible challenges us, as it has challenged countless generations, concerning what we do and think, who we are and how we live. Are we ready to listen and respond?

Never be afraid to ask God questions, but never close your ears to the questions he wants to ask you in turn.

90   Making whole

Readings   Mark 2:1-12; 5:1-13; Luke 10:38-42

Aim   To illustrate that Jesus brought healing of body, mind and spirit during his ministry, and to show also that we are called to share in bringing wholeness to others.

Preparation   On A3-sized pieces of paper, copy the three simple pictures below (larger versions suitable for photocopying may be found in the Photocopy Masters section on pages 322-323). Label these in bold letters as shown (Jesus heals the paralysed man; Jesus ministers to Martha and Mary; Jesus heals Legion). Cut each of the labelled pictures into eight pieces, fix magnetic tape or blutack and then jumble the pieces of all three pictures together.

Jesus heals the paralysed man

Jesus ministers to Martha and Mary

Jesus heals Legion

Talk   Tell the congregation that you have prepared three pictures illustrating the healing ministry of Jesus, but that these have become jumbled up. Ask three volunteers to come forward and help sort out the pieces and put the pictures back together again.

The healing ministry of Jesus wasn't, of course, anything like as simple as that, but there is one thing that both had in common, for just as we reassembled the pictures, so Jesus helped put broken lives back together again throughout his ministry. For the paralysed man, it was healing of body; for Martha, it was healing of the mind, helping her to discover the secret of inner peace amid the bustle of daily life; for Legion, it was healing of the spirit, the storm within calmed so that he was at peace with himself and with God.

Wholeness of body, mind and spirit – that is what God desires for each one of us, and it is a ministry in which we are called to share, not in sensational acts of healing, but in simple acts of love and kindness, care and acceptance, solidarity and support. Not that all those suffering from physical or mental illness are always healed, for there is much in this world that will always frustrate God's purpose, but even in pain and sickness we believe he can bring strength, support and tranquillity of spirit; a wholeness now that is a foretaste of the blessing and fulfilment he promises in the life to come.

91   Reshaped!

Reading   Luke 4:16-21

Aim   This talk, using a similar idea to that in the last, aims to show how God, through Christ, is able to reshape our lives, giving them new meaning and direction.

Preparation   For this talk you will need a simple Lego® model of a person. Practise putting this together until you are able to do it speedily and efficiently. Then, assemble the various pieces instead into a haphazard shape, and display at the front of the church ready for the beginning of the talk.

Talk   Hold up your 'model' and ask if anyone can tell you what it is? Rearrange the pieces to form the Lego® person. (You might like to involve young people in doing this, perhaps showing them a copy of the instructions for making the model.) Hold up the finished model and ask if anyone can see what it is now.

In a sense what we have seen here is echoed time and time again in the biblical stories about Jesus, only what he was reshaping there was not Lego® bricks but human lives. There were Matthew and Zacchaeus, both tax collectors, their lives changed forever once they met him. There was Nicodemus, a Pharisee, who, having first come to Jesus by night, was later to ask Pilate for Jesus' body. There was the woman caught in adultery, and the woman of Samaria, the rich young man, those with leprosy, those who couldn't walk and those who couldn't see, the troubled in body, mind and spirit – these, and countless others who came to Jesus with their lives in a mess and who went away reshaped, renewed, refashioned, redeemed.

Suddenly they could see a pattern and a purpose where before there had been confusion; suddenly their lives made sense.

And that is as true today as ever, as countless people still experience the transforming power of Christ. What of us? Is everything in our life what it could and should be? Or are we confused, searching for something to give it meaning? The promise of Jesus is as much for you and me as anyone; he waits only for us to seek his help before reshaping our lives in turn.

92   Wiping away our tears

Readings   Psalm 6; Revelation 21:1-4

Aim   This talk explores the theme of sorrow, something we can shy away from when talking to young people but an issue that affects us all and needs to be faced.

Preparation   For this talk you will need an onion, a plate, a knife and a cardboard box! Place the knife on the plate, and place this in turn in the box. To avoid any possibility of accidents, be careful not to leave it unattended. You may also want a bowl of soapy water to wash your hands afterwards!

Talk   Tell the congregation that you have something very sad to show them, so sad that you've hidden it inside a box for fear of having them all in tears. Ask if anyone would like to see what it is, and, as volunteers come forward, reach into the box, take the knife and slice the onion up. Each volunteer, after looking inside, will probably go away smiling. Express surprise, and tell the congregation that despite their apparent amusement, the item inside the box has brought tears to *your* eyes if no one else's. Lift the plate out of the box, to reveal the onion, playing up the idea of a poor defenceless onion cruelly chopped to pieces.

There is, of course, nothing sad in the box after all, and of course there are many things in life that bring tears to our eyes apart from sadness. We speak sometimes about tears of joy, crying for happiness, and we can shed tears similarly in any time of high emotion.

Yet if joy is very much part of human life, each of us will at some time also experience the tragedy and the sorrow that goes with it. Faith needs to be able to make sense of and speak to such situations as much as to any other. And that's precisely what we see in our readings today. 'I am tired of my misery,' writes David in the Psalms (6:6-7, own translation); 'every night I soak my bed with tears; I saturate my couch with my weeping. My eyes waste away because of sorrow; they grow feeble because of all my enemies.'

Here is a cry from the heart, a readiness to bring his sorrow and despair to God, just as at other times he brings his praise and thanksgiving. God, he knows, is willing to accept both, and, equally, he *will* respond, bringing light out of darkness, hope out of despair, laughter out of tears. As David writes in another of his Psalms (30:5, own translation), 'Tears may linger for the night, but joy dawns in the morning.' In other words, sorrow will never be allowed to have the last word. However much it may not seem like it at the time, God's love and light will shine through. And so David ends that

Psalm we looked at earlier with words of thanksgiving: 'The Lord has heard the sound of my weeping. The Lord has heard my supplication; the Lord accepts my prayer' (Psalm 6:8b-9). And though the pain of some sorrow is never forgotten in this life, we look forward as Christians to the time when tears will be no more – the time looked forward to in those wonderful words from the book of Revelation (21:3b-4): 'See, the home of God is among mortals. He will dwell with them; they will be his peoples, and God himself will be with them; he will wipe every tear from their eyes. Death will be no more; mourning and crying and pain will be no more, for the first things have passed away.'

93   Pulling our weight

Reading   1 Corinthians 12:4-26

Aim   To emphasise that the contribution each of us can make to God's kingdom is important, and to ask if we are doing our bit.

Preparation   For this talk you will need a strong rope and plenty of space! You will also need some volunteers to take part in a tug of war contest. (Do not attempt this talk if there is a danger of participants in the tug of war falling on to concrete or hitting their heads against pews, furniture, etc.) It is probably best to choose teams beforehand, so that you can ensure these are more or less balanced.

Talk   Tell the congregation that you have organised a tug of war contest, and ask your two teams to come forward. Ask at the beginning which team the congregation thinks will win, and then see if they are right. (If no result is achieved after a minute or so, call the contest a draw.) Ask the strongest-looking member of the winning team (or of either team if the contest was drawn) to join the other side, and then hold the contest again. (In the unlikely event that the same team wins again, remove another participant from that team and hold a third contest.)

On their own, no participants would be able to do very much but when part of a team they can all pull together to good effect. Take one person out, and everybody in the team suffers. The same would be true if that person simply stopped pulling their weight, standing there but simply making up the numbers.

The same is true with being a Christian. God needs all of us to work together in his service. Alone, there is a limit to what we can do, but when we work together as a church or with other Christians, then we can all be part of something much bigger. Are we doing that? Are we playing our part, pulling our weight, sharing the load, or are we leaving it to others to do the work? Each of us has something to contribute. How many of us are doing so?

94 Silent but present

Reading Job 30:16-31

Aim To explain that though prayers sometimes do not seem to be answered, and though God may feel far away, he is present and involved in our situation, even when we do not see him.

Preparation On separate slips of card/paper, print the following in large bold letters:

PNEUMONIA, GNOME, KNICKERBOCKER, MNEMONIC, SCIATICA, HONORARIUM, PSYCHOLOGICAL, WHOLE, DIAPHRAGM, NUMB

Affix a piece of blutack to the back of each, and put them aside for use later in the talk.

Talk Tell the congregation that you have a spelling test for them. Read out the words you have printed, and ask who can spell them. Take a vote each time as to the correct spelling, and then display this on a whiteboard.

When you have gone through the list, ask what the words have in common. The answer, of course, is that all have a silent letter or letters in them; letters, in other words, that, although present, are neither pronounced nor heard in speech.

The book of Job shows us something similar, although the context is altogether different. Job cries out in distress, begging for help, yet no matter how often he prays or how earnestly he pleads, God seems strangely distant. Unsurprisingly, Job couldn't understand why his prayers apparently weren't answered, and things reached the point when he decided that God must have abandoned him. Yet the book ends on a very different note, Job coming to recognise that though he had been unaware of it, God had been with him all along, silent but present.

For us, in turn, there will be times when God seems close, intimately involved in our lives, speaking his word directly and clearly, but there will be times also when we search for him in vain, when we call out but he doesn't seem to answer. Never forget that, though we may not be aware of it, he is present in our world and present in our lives, recognised or unrecognised, working out his purpose.

95   Spot the difference

Reading   Romans 12:1-2

Aim   To bring home the fact that commitment to Christ should make a difference to the way we live.

Preparation   Copy and enlarge the following pictures (larger versions may be found in the Photocopy Masters section on pages 324-325). Display them on two large whiteboards, side by side.

Talk   Display the two pictures and ask who can spot the 11 differences between them. Involve as many people in giving the answers as possible. (The differences in the second picture are as follows: different pattern on flag; different time on clock; different-shaped side door; crossed bars on side window; horizontal bar on window too low; different-size and shaped cloud; missing bird; handle different on right door; person's arms raised; roof tiles missing, door handle on side door.)

At first sight, both pictures look the same, but a closer look reveals that there are many small but significant differences. There's a parallel here with being a Christian. To follow Christ should make a difference to our lives. So Paul writes in his letter to the church in Rome: 'Do not be conformed to the spirit of the age, but transformed by the renewing of your mind, so that your life might attest to the good, well-pleasing and perfect will of God' (Romans 12:2, own translation). That doesn't mean we look any different on the outside, nor that we need be thought odd or unusual in a negative sense, but it does mean that something about Christ should set us apart, something in the quality of our love, the sincerity of our relationships, the integrity of our dealings, the attitude we have towards life.

'What difference does it make?' – that's what people will ask us concerning faith in Christ. Answers to that in words have their place, but the most effective answer will always be if people can look at who we are and spot the difference for themselves.

96   The God who sees in secret

Readings   Psalm 94:8-11; Matthew 6:5-6; Hebrews 4:12-16

Aim   To bring home the fact that nothing is hidden from God.

Preparation   No special preparation is needed for this talk.

Talk   Tell the congregation that you can read their minds! To prove it, ask them to take part in this simple exercise:

- Think of a number between 1 and 10
- Multiply that number by 9
- If the resulting number is a two-digit number, add the digits together
- Take away four
- Assuming 1 = A, 2 = B, 3 = C and so on, identify the letter your number corresponds to, but don't tell anyone.
- Think of a book in the New Testament beginning with that letter
- Think of one of the Apostles whose name begins with the last letter of that New Testament book.
- You are thinking of Ephesians and Simon Peter!

Am I able to read minds? Of course not! It looks like it, but there's a trick in the numbers. Try it yourself at home and see. With God, though, it's different. He *does* know what we are thinking, for he sees not just the outside but the inside, not just what we do but what we are thinking, not just what we say but what we feel. As Psalm 94 puts it (v. 11), 'The Lord knows our thoughts, that they are but an empty breath.' Or, as the writer of the book of Hebrews (4:12) says, still more bluntly, 'The word of God . . . is able to judge the thoughts and intentions of the heart.'

We cannot, then, pretend with God. We can't conceal our faults or disguise our weaknesses. Thankfully, we don't have to, for having shared our humanity in Christ, experienced the same testing and temptations, he accepts us by his grace, asking only that we acknowledge our mistakes and seek his forgiveness.

97   Setting us free

Readings   John 8:31-47; Romans 7:14-25

Aim   To show that, in Christ, God offers us freedom from all that prevents us living life to the full.

Preparation   For this talk you will need 22 lengths of thick twine/cord or strips of fabric, and a pair of scissors. You will also need a chair placed in a prominent position at the front of the church.

Finally, you will also need the following words, printed in large bold letters on separate strips of card/paper:

FREESTANDING, FREEHAND, FREE RANGE, FREEPOST, FREE DROP, FREE COUNTRY, FREE GIFT, FREEHOLD, FREE WILL, FREE KICK, FREEWHEEL, FREE FOR ALL, FREESTYLE, FREE SPEECH, FREE ENTERPRISE, FREEWAY, FREE PERIOD, FREE HOUSE, FREE FALL, FREE PARKING, FREELANCE, FREE PAPER

Talk   Ask for some volunteers to help with the talk. Get one person to sit in the chair you've positioned at the front of the church, and ask the others to help you tie this person up using the 22 cords. Announce that the only way the unfortunate captive can be set free is for the congregation to answer the 'quiz' you've prepared for them. Explain that all the answers have the word FREE in them. (For added effect you might like to print out the questions and attach one to each of the lengths of cord). As each question is answered correctly, cut one of the cords tying your captive (taking care not to injure him or her in the process!) The quiz clues are as follows (arrange the answers on a whiteboard, as set out afterwards):

1. Needs no support *FREESTANDING*
2. A way of drawing or sketching *FREEHAND*
3. Eggs that don't come from a factory farm *FREE RANGE*
4. This means you can send a letter at no charge *FREEPOST*
5. Allowed this sometimes in a game of golf *FREE DROP*
6. England, Spain, France, Germany are all examples of this *FREE COUNTRY*
7. Something often given to encourage us to buy something else *FREE GIFT*
8. May see this on a 'For Sale' notice *FREEHOLD*
9. The right and ability to choose or otherwise *FREE WILL*
10. Something awarded for a foul in a game of football *FREE KICK*
11. You can do this on a bike but shouldn't do when driving a car *FREEWHEEL*

12. A time when anything goes *FREE FOR ALL*
13. Doing things in one's own way; a type of swimming *FREESTYLE*
14. Means we can all say what we like *FREE SPEECH*
15. Taking risks to set up one's own business or company *FREE ENTERPRISE*
16. American word for main road or motorway *FREEWAY*
17. Something you might possibly get at school if a teacher is unwell *FREE PERIOD*
18. A pub not owned by a particular brewery *FREE HOUSE*
19. Something you might do before opening a parachute (as well as pray!) *FREE FALL*
20. Something you can't ever find when in your car *FREE PARKING*
21. Someone who works for themselves *FREELANCE*
22. Something we get through the door but rarely read! *FREE PAPER*

```
            F R E E S T A N D I N G
            F R E E H A N D
    F R E E     R A N G E

        F R E E P O S T
        F R E E     D R O P
        F R E E     C O U N T R Y
      F R E E     G I F T
            F R E E H O L D

          F R E E     W I L L
        F R E E     K I C K
      F R E E W H E E L
    F R E E     F O R     A L L

            F R E E S T Y L E
      F R E E     S P E E C H
        F R E E     E N T E R P R I S E

          F R E E W A Y
      F R E E     P E R I O D
        F R E E     H O U S E

          F R E E     F A L L
        F R E E     P A R K I N G
      F R E E L A N C E
      F R E E     P A P E R
```

As the last length of cord is cut, thank your 'prisoner' and your other helpers for their assistance.

Setting our captive free proved a long business, but, as anyone who has ever tried kicking a habit, conquering a weakness, or overcoming a disability will be all too aware, securing our freedom from much that holds us captive in life can be harder still. If so, the words of the Apostle Paul to the Romans will strike a chord with us, for they sum up the frustration we can feel at being unable to live and act in the way we, at least in our better moments, would wish.

> I'm a slave instead to the flesh and to sin. I do not understand why I act as I do. For I end up doing the things I despise rather than the things I yearn to do . . . I know what I ought to do, but however much I intend to do it, evil invariably gains the upper hand. It has to be down to that power of sin deep within . . . for though I take heartfelt delight in the law of God, part of me seems to feel differently, my mind somehow held captive to the law of sin that dwells in my members. What a miserable creature I am! Can anyone set me free from this body of death? Thanks be to God, he has done so through Jesus Christ. I am, though, still torn between the old and new self, the way of God and the way of flesh, but he has acted to make me new (Romans 7:14a-15, 17-20, 22-25; own paraphrase).

Is there any solution to our predicament, any way to set us free? At one time Paul had seen the answer in terms of following the Law, but somehow, however hard he tried, true freedom evaded him; until, that is, he heard and responded to the gospel:

> Can anyone set me free from this body of death? Thanks be to God, he has done so through Jesus Christ. I am, though, still torn between the old and new self, the way of God and the way of flesh, but he has acted to make me new (Romans 7:24b-25; own paraphrase).

Here, says Paul, is the answer, an answer that is at once incredibly simple and yet awesomely wonderful. We don't earn our freedom. It is the gift of God in Christ. Through Christ, God delivers us from everything that imprisons us, that prevents us from living life to the full. We don't suddenly become perfect, but we are accepted as we are, offered forgiveness, and given the opportunity to begin again, not just in our own strength but in God's. Through him we find mercy, love, hope, peace, new life; in other words, freedom from guilt, hatred, despair, anxiety and even death itself. As Jesus so wonderfully put it in words recorded by John (8:31, 36; own translation): 'Jesus said, "If you continue in my word, truly living as my disciples, then you will know the truth and the truth will set you free . . . If the Son frees you from captivity, you will indeed be free."'

And that, as you've probably noticed, is the message that comes across from our quiz (point to the hidden message concealed in the answers): THE TRUTH WILL SET YOU FREE. All we need do is respond to what God has already done. Have we discovered the freedom he offers us in Christ?

98   The missing piece

Reading   Luke 10:38-42; 18:18-22

Aim   To bring home that without Christ something vital is missing from our lives.

Preparation   In large bold letters print the following and arrange them on a whiteboard.

As light as a . . .
2 + 2 + 1 = 14
Red, orange, yellow, green, indigo, violet
This is the hose that Jack built
Its a hard one this
This one's hard to
A, B, C, D, F, G, H
England, Northern Ireland, Wales
The result was a forgone conclusion
Ringo Starr, John Lennon, George Harrison
Mercury, Venus, Mars, Jupiter, Saturn, Uranus, Neptune, Pluto
Henry VII, Henry VIII, Edward VI, Elizabeth I
Can you solve this one

Talk   Show the congregation the display and ask if anyone can spot what each entry has in common. The answer, of course, is that all have something vital missing from them. Go through the list one by one, asking what is missing in each case (answers are given in italics)

As light as a *feather*
2 + 2 + *10* = 14
Red, orange, yellow, green, *blue,* indigo, violet
This is the ho*u*se that Jack built
It's a hard one this
This one's hard to*o*
A, B, C, D, *E,* F, G, H
England, Northern Ireland, Wales, *Scotland*
The result was a for*e*gone conclusion
Ringo Starr, John Lennon, George Harrison, *Paul McCartney*
Mercury, Venus, *Earth,* Mars, Jupiter, Saturn, Uranus, Neptune, Pluto
Henry VII, Henry VIII, Edward VI, *Mary I,* Elizabeth I
Can you solve this one*?*

All of these without the missing word, letter, person, object or punctuation were incomplete; there was something vital missing. And the same was true, though in a slightly different sense, for two people in our reading. The first was Martha, sister of Mary; the second was the rich ruler who came to Jesus asking about eternal life. Both had something missing in their lives, something that left them feeling incomplete.

In Martha's case, she was probably unaware of the empty gap in her life, even while she ran around trying to fill it. It took Jesus to confront her with the situation to make her face up to reality. 'The Lord answered her, "Martha, Martha, you are fretting and distracted by many things; only one thing is really important. Mary has chosen that more important thing, and it will not be taken away from her"' (Luke 10:40-42, own translation).

The case of the rich ruler is even more striking, for here is a man who on the surface had everything: riches, comfort, security – just the sort of things we so often strive for today. Yet he realised that he couldn't take these with him when he died, and clearly felt a hollowness within as a result. 'What should I do to receive eternal life?' he asked (Luke 18:18b, own translation). The answer Jesus gave seems illogical. 'You still lack one thing. Sell all you have and give the proceeds to the poor, and you will discover treasure in heaven. Then come and follow me' (Luke 18:22b, own translation). Before receiving he had to let go. To make room for what mattered he had to discard what was unimportant.

What, then, of us? Our lives may be full and rich yet still feel as though something is missing. We may have much to give thanks for, yet still be searching for the one link to pull it all together. Without God, our lives are incomplete. We need a spiritual dimension, an experience of the love of Christ and an openness to his will if life is to make sense and be lived to the full.

99 Making it known

Reading   Matthew 5:13-16; 28:16-20

Aim   To ask whether we are getting our message across as Christians, and whether the claims we make are substantiated by the lives we live.

Preparation   No special preparation is needed for this talk, though you may like to print the clues and answers to add a visual element to the talk. You might also like to add other more recent advertisements.

Talk   Ask how many people watch TV commercials and how many take any notice of them. Tell the congregation that you have some recently used advertising slogans, and that you want to see how effective these have been in getting the advertisers' message across and their product noticed. Run through the following clues, asking if anyone can identify the company in question:

- The future is (*Orange*)
- More connections, more possibilities (*BT*)
- Exclusively for everyone (*Marks & Spencer*)
- Stamping down on prices (*PC World*)
- Say it with flowers (*Interflora*)
- You can do it if you _ _ _ it (*B&Q*)
- Start here, go anywhere (*Halfords*)
- Loves the jobs you hate (*Mr Muscle*)
- Does exactly what it says on the tin (*Ronseal*)
- Perfection in confection (*Thorntons*)
- Bags more for your money (*Iceland*)
- You want it. We've got it (*Staples*)

Each of these slogans was designed to publicise a company and its product. How effective are we in getting across our message in comparison. We are not, of course, selling or pushing a product but, like the first disciples, we are called to proclaim Christ and to make known the gospel so that others might hear and respond to it for themselves. How successful are you in communicating your faith. How effectual in leading others to consider the claims of Christ?

Not that we can win people to faith through words alone. No matter how clever they might be, words must be backed up by substance, just as advertising finally depends on how far the product advertised measures up to the claims made for it. Any words we speak, then, must be reinforced by action. As Jesus told the multitude in the Sermon on the Mount: 'You are the light of the world. Just as a city situated on a mountaintop cannot be hidden, so nobody lights a lamp and places it under a bushel basket, putting it instead on a lamp-stand in order that it might shed light throughout the house. Similarly, let your light shine before others, so that they may see the good deeds you do and give glory to your Father in heaven' (Matthew 5:14-16, own translation). Is that true of us? Does the way we live tally with the people we claim to be? Do our deeds speak as powerfully as our words? Does either speak of Christ at all? We may not all be evangelists but we are called to be witnesses, each given the responsibility of making Christ known.

100   Christian clothing

Readings   Ephesians 6:10-11, 14-15, 17; Colossians 3:12-14

Aim   To ask whether what we are on the inside measures up to what we claim to be on the outside.

Preparation   Giving plenty of advance notice, ask children to come to the service in fancy dress as one of the following: milkman, postwoman, station-master, choirboy, vicar, policewoman, judge, nun, mayor, firefighter, soldier, footballer, traffic warden, chef, etc. If you do not have enough children in your church to make this viable, ask children (and per-haps adults too) to draw pictures of these people – this should be fun in itself, seeing if anyone can guess what these are meant to represent! Alternatively, you might use a cheap pack of 'Happy Families' playing cards, many versions of which depict characters such as the above. If you choose this latter option, you will need to cover over the names with sticky paper, and invite volunteers to come to the front, so that they can see the picture on the cards.

Talk   Parade your fancy dress volunteers (or display the pre-prepared drawings/playing cards, depending on the option you choose), and ask who can identify the occupation of each character. Ask how we are able to know. In each case, we can recognise the job or vocation of the person concerned immediately, simply by what he or she wears. But of course, though the clothes tell us what these people do, they don't tell us much about the individuals underneath: about their temperament, characters or personalities. Clothes can tell us a little about people, but ultimately it's what's on the inside rather than the outside that matters. The Bible has a lot to say on this subject, talking in many places about what we might call Christian clothing.

First, the Old Testament: 'The Lord has anointed me,' says the prophet Isaiah, '. . . to provide for those who mourn in Zion – to give them a garland instead of ashes . . . he has clothed me with the garments of salvation, he has covered me with the robe of righteous-ness' (61:1b, 3a, 10b). In the New Testament, there is much more. There's the first letter of Peter, for example (5:5b: 'All of you must clothe yourselves with humility in your dealings with one another.' And, of course, there's the words of the Apostle Paul. 'Put on the full armour of God,' he says to the Ephesians (6:11, 14-15, 17, own translation). 'Don the whole armour of God, so that you may be able to withstand the ruses of the devil. Stand resolute, and secure the belt of truth around your waist, and put on the breastplate of righteousness. Shoe your feet with a readiness to proclaim the gospel of peace. In addition, put on the helmet of salvation, and the sword of the Spirit, which is the word of God.' 'All who have been baptised in Christ have been clothed with him,' he tells the Galatians (3:27, own translation). 'Clothe yourselves with the Lord Jesus Christ,' he writes to the Romans (13:14). The message is summed up in his words to the church in Colossae: 'As God's chosen ones, therefore, holy and greatly loved, clothe yourselves with compassion, kindness, humility, gentleness and patience, being merciful to one another and forgiving any quarrel you may have; in other words, forgive as the Lord forgave you. Above all, clothe yourselves with love, which binds everything together in perfect harmony' (Colossians 3:12-14, own translation).

These, then, are the 'clothes' we should wear as Christians: compassion, kindness, humility, gentleness, patience, mercy, love, truth and righteousness. You can't buy clothes like these in any shop. They come from God. They are not clothes that we put on and off as the whim takes us; rather, they are qualities that should clothe our lives always. And though these clothes will not tell anyone about the sort of job we do, they should tell them something far more important: about the faith we have and the God we serve, for if we exhibit these in our lives, then they will speak unmistakably of Christ and his power at work within us.

INDEXES

Subject Index

(References are to talk rather than page numbers)

action, faith seen in 35, 50-52, 68,
    77, 95, 99
Advent 1-6
All Saints' Day 40-41
allegiance, to Christ 19
ambassadors, for Christ 68
anniversary, church 63-65
Ascension, of Christ 33-34

barriers between us and God,
    broken down in Christ 78
Bible, knowing it better 3-4
Blockbusters 16
builders, wise and foolish 73

call of God 84
Cana, wedding feast at 14
changed lives 6, 18, 75
choices 16-17
Christian Aid 50-52
    see also global justice
Christian unity 45-47
Christian,
    characteristics of 35, 75, 77,
    95, 100
Christmas 7-12
Church
    membership and
      fellowship of 66-68, 93
    nature of 41, 63-64
    unity of 45-47
commitment 19, 71
confessing our faith 71
cost, paid by God to
    redeem us 12, 26
creative power of God 56-57, 76
cross
    meekness and majesty
      seen in 27
    victory of 29
    see also Easter

death, conquered by life 29-30
decisions, moral 16-17
despair, turned to hope 28-30
diversity, unity in 45-47
doubt, turned to faith 28-31, 89

Easter 29-32
eating together 79
Epiphany 13-14
Eucharist 79
evil, confronting 62
examination, spiritual 23
eye of faith 72

faith
    confession of 71
    questions of 89
    restored 28-31
    seen in action 35, 50-52, 68,
    77, 95, 99
    seeing with eye of 72
faithfulness of God,
    in Christ 42-43, 85
fathers 53-54
faults, acknowledging 20, 22, 23,
    78, 96
fear, turned to trust 28, 30
fellowship of Church, working
    together within 66-67, 93
    see also unity
forgiveness 6, 21, 44, 75, 96
foundations, firm 73
freedom
    in Christ 81, 97
    limits on 87
friendship, offered by Jesus 85
fruits, of the Spirit 37, 100
fulfilment, true nature of 98
future, trusting God for 42-43

global justice 50-52, 55, 57
glory, of Christ 34
good news
    responding to 5, 7-9, 11, 71
    sharing 10, 32
grace 6, 21, 44, 75, 96
greatness and wonder of God
    revealed in Ascension
      of Christ 33-34
    revealed through the
      Trinity 38-39
    see also creative power of God;
      strength, in weakness
guidance of God 42-43, 48-49, 84

Harvest thanksgiving 55-57
healing and wholeness 90
Herod 7
Holy Communion 79
Holy Spirit – gift, fruits
    and work of 35-37
Holy Week 26-28
honesty, in prayer 83
humanity and divinity
    of Christ 27, 33-34
humility, of Christ 27
hungry, the 57
    see also Christian Aid

idolatry, modern forms of 82
image, creating God in
    our own 82
innkeeper 7

John the Baptist 1-2, 5, 10, 16, 18
Joseph, husband of Mary 5, 7-8
joy, from sorrow 28-30, 88, 92
justice, global 50-52, 55, 57

kingdom of God 2, 24-25
kingship of Christ 24-25, 27

laughter 88
Lent 15-23
life, from death 92
light
    of the world, Christ as 13
    letting ours shine before
      others 77, 99
Lord's Supper 79
love, of God 48-49, 53-54, 78

magi 5, 7, 8
Martha and Mary 98
Mary, mother of Jesus 5, 7-8, 11-12
meal, sharing in 79
membership,
    of Church 66-68, 93
mercy 6, 21, 44, 75, 96
mistakes,
    acknowledging 20, 22, 23, 78, 96
mothers 48-49
music, worshipping through 69-70

neighbours, responding to 50
new beginnings 42-44
new creation, in Christ 18, 44, 91
New Year 42-44
Nicodemus 36

Old and New Year 42-44
ordinary, transformed by God 14
otherness of God,
    expressed through doctrine
      of the Trinity 38-39

Palm Sunday 24-25
pancakes 15
parables 72
peace, global 58, 61-62
Pentecost 35-37
perseverance 40
pondering the good news 11
power of God 74, 86

see also greatness and
  wonder of God
prayer
  honesty in   83
  when seems unanswered   94
  preparing, for return of Christ   1
  purpose of God   84

questions of faith   89

reflecting, upon good news   11
Remembrance Day   61-62
repentance   18, 20, 21
  see also mistakes,
    acknowledging
representatives of Christ   68
resolutions, New Year   44
responding, to good news
  of the gospel   5, 7-9, 11, 71
resurrection   29-32
return of Christ
  preparing for   1
  signs of   2
rich ruler   98
right and wrong, deciding
  between   16-17

saints, nature and
  characteristics of   40-41

Samuel, God's call to   84
Second Coming
  preparing for   1
  signs of   2
secret, God who sees in   96
self-interest   80
sensitivity, towards consciences
  and weaknesses of others   87
service, offering to God rather
  than self   80
shepherds, response
  to Christ   7, 8, 10
Shrove Tuesday   15
signs, of return of Christ   2
Simeon   12
social responsibility   50-52, 55, 57
songs of praise   69-70
sorrow, turned to joy 28-30, 88, 92
Spirit – gift, fruits and
  work of   35-37
stewardship, of God's gifts   15
strength, in weakness   74, 86

temptation   16-17, 21
Transfiguration   34
transforming power
  of God   6, 14, 28-31, 74, 86, 91
Trinity, nature of   38-39
trust   42-43, 48-49
truth, setting us free   97

unanswered prayer   94
unity
  in Christ   66-67
  of Church   45-47
  global   58-60
unseen, faith in   36, 94

voice of God   84

war   61-62
water, into wine   14
way, truth and life, Jesus as   81
weakness, God's strength in 74, 86
wholeness, inner   90
wine, water turned into
  by Jesus   14
wise and foolish builders   73
witnesses, cloud of   40-41, 65
witnessing, to Christ   10, 32, 99
wonder of God
  revealed in Ascension
    of Christ   33-34
  revealed through
    the Trinity   38-39
Word, made flesh   3-4
world, interdependent
  nature of   55, 58-60
worship, through music
  and song   69-70

Index of Main Bible Passages

(References are to talk rather than page numbers)

Genesis
11:1-9	59
22:8a	49

Deuteronomy
4:9a	62
4:23a	62
6:4-9	61
8:11a	62

Joshua
1:9	48
24:14-28	19

1 Samuel
3:2-10	84

2 Samuel
12:1-7	20
23:1-7	24

Job
3:11, 20-21a	83
30:16-31	94

Psalms
6	92
10:1	83
13:1-2	83
16:1	49
18:41	57
22:1-2	83
24	60
26:2	23
30	88
30:5	92
31:9-24	48
32:8a	49
37:23-24	48
46:1	49
51:1-12	6
65:1, 9-13	56
66:16-20	83
67:6	57
73:23-24a	48
74:1	83
94:2-3	83
94:8-11	96
96:1-9	70
98	69
100:5	49
103:2	62
104:1-30	55
104:14-15, 28	48
106:10, 13a, 21	62
116	42
119:83b, 93, 109b	62
119:105-112	3
139:13-18	76
145	57

Proverbs
2:1-15	89
3:1	62
3:11	49
3:11-12	48
4:5	62
8:32	48
16:18-19	80
17:17	85
27:6, 10	85

Isaiah
1:12-20	6
9:6-7	25
35:3	49
35:4b	49
40:1-11	1
40:10a, 11	48
40:11a	49
40:18-26	38
41:13	48
42:5-9	48
46:1-10	82
46:5-7	38
49:1-6	76
51:13a	62
52:5-10	9
58:11a	49
61:1b, 3a, 10b	100
66:13	48, 49

Jeremiah
2:32b	62
3:21	62
29:10-14	43
31:28b	49

Ezekiel
34:16	48

Hosea
6:1	49

Joel
2:26	57

Matthew
1:18-25	6
2:1-12	8, 13
3:13-4:22	16
5:13-16	77, 99
5:43-48	77
6:5-6	96
6:28-30	48
7:7-8	89
7:24-27	73
10:27-31	26
11:2-27	2
12:33-37	17
13:1-17	72
13:31-32	74
18:20	66
25:1-46	51
25:31-46	52
26:72	28
28:1-20	32
28:16-20	99

Mark
1:1-8	5, 18
2:1-12	90
5:1-13	90
15:16-39	27
16:1-14	34
16:8	28

Luke
1:57-79	1
2:1-7	7
2:1-16	8
2:8-14	9
2:8-18	10
2:8-19	11
2:25-35	12
4:1-13	21
4:16-21	91
6:20-21	88
9:21-27	71
10:25-37	50
10:38-42	90, 98
12:28	49
12:42-48	15
15:11-32	53
15:17	57
17:5-6	74
18:18-22	98
19:36-38	25
19:37	28
22:14-23	61, 79
22:45	28
24:13-35	31
24:50-53	33

John
1:1-5	13
1:6-9	10

1:10-13   7
1:14   34
1:14-18   3
2:1-11   14
3:1-15   36
3:13-21   60
3:16-21   26
8:12   13
8:31, 36   97
12:16   28
12:27   28
14:1-7   81
14:27b   28
15:12-17   85
17:1-26   59
17:20-23   64
18:33-37   24, 25
19:12-16   24
20:1-29   29, 30
20:30-31   4

Acts
1:6-11   34
2:38-47   67
11:19-26   75

Romans
5:8   22
7:14-25   97
8:12-17   54
10:5-13   58
12:1-2   95
13:14   100

1 Corinthians
1:1-3   41
8:1-13   87

9:24-26   40
10:23-11:1   87
12:1-12   36
12:1-13, 27-31   46
12:4-6, 12-13 45, 47
12:4-26   93
14:1-19   37

2 Corinthians
4:18   36
5:11-21   68
5:16-21   18, 44
9:8   57
13:5-10   23
13:13   38

Galatians
1:13, 22-23   29
3:23-29   58
3:27   100
5:13-26   35
5:16-26   23, 37

Ephesians
2:1-22   63
2:11-22   41, 64
2:13-18   78
3:16-21   39
4:1-6   54
4:15-16   46
5:15-20   70
6:10-11,14-15, 17 100

Philippians
2:1-11   80
4:10-14   86

Colossians
2:1-6   66
2:6-7   19
2:13-15   78
3:5-11   78
3:11   58
3:12-14   100
3:16-17   69

1 Timothy
6:13-16   25

Hebrews
4:12-16   96
4:14-16   21
12:1-2   40
13:7-8   65

James
1:17   48
1:22-27   52
1:25   62
2:14-17   52

1 Peter
2:1-10   63
2:9-10   75
5:5b   100
5:7   49

1 John
1:5-10   17, 20
1:9a   49

Revelation
21:1-4   43, 92
21:23b-25   13

PHOTOCOPY MASTERS

Chicken pox

Flu

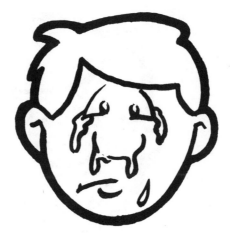

Mumps

Toothache

Measles

Scarlet fever

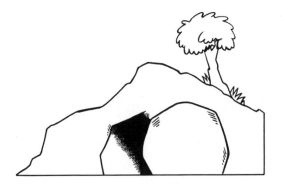

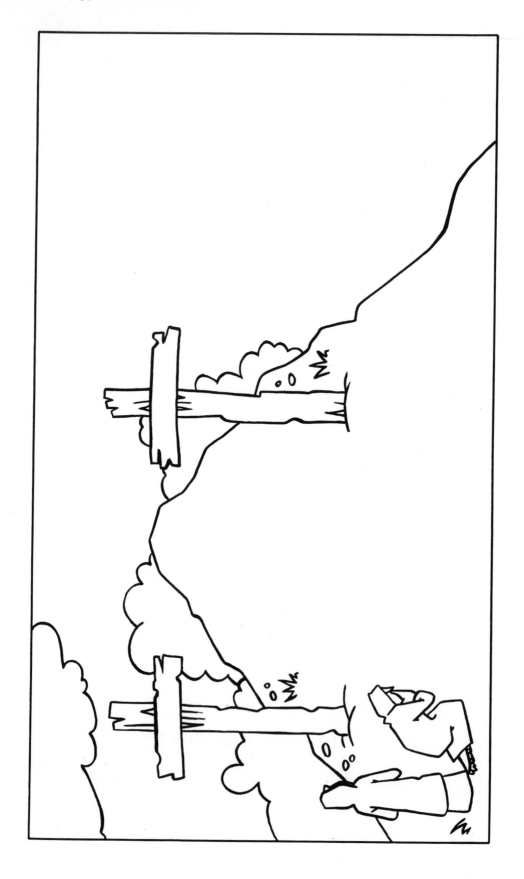

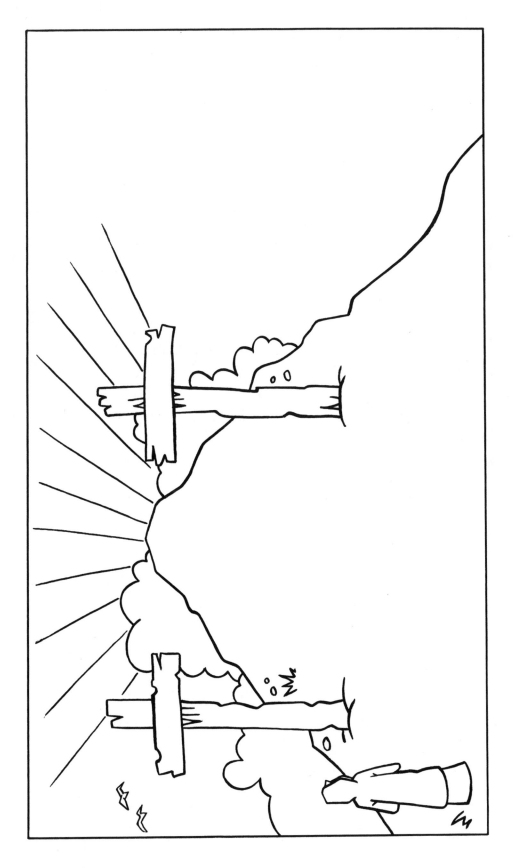

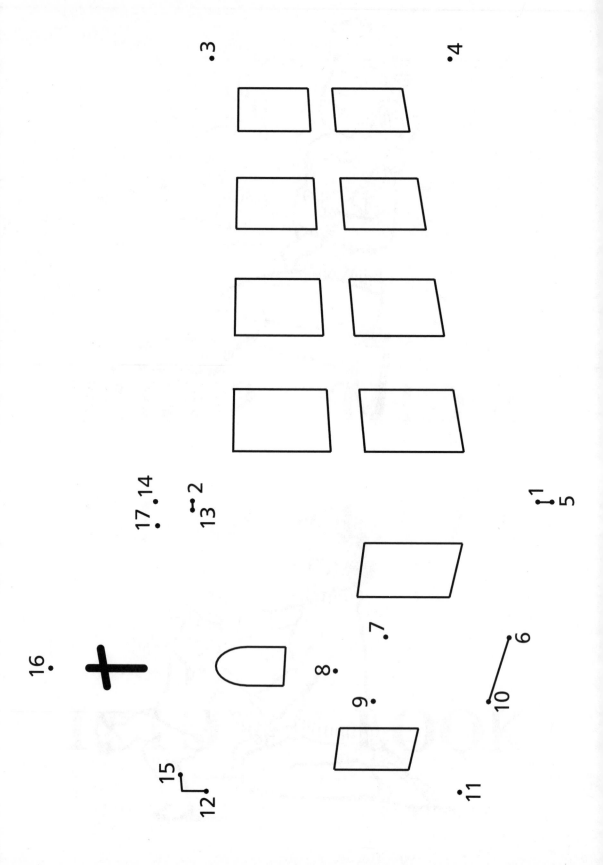

LOOK BEFORE YOU LEAP

SIGHT	SIGHT
SIGHT	SIGHT

FORESIGHT

| ꓘOOˍ | CI2I |

LOOK THE OTHER WAY   SEE EYE TO EYE

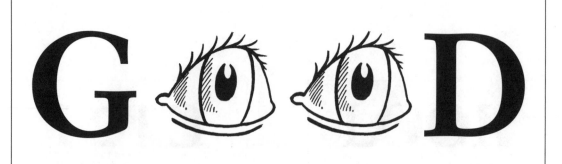

VISION VISION

I

I 4 I

X I'D

SELF

SELF-CENTRED

CONCEITED IDIOT

PRIDE GOES BEFORE A FALL

2**4**1, 1, 1, BOOTS

TOO BIG FOR ONE'S BOOTS

1 LOOKING

LOOKING AFTER NUMBER ONE

BIG-HEADED

BLOWING ONE'S OWN TRUMPET

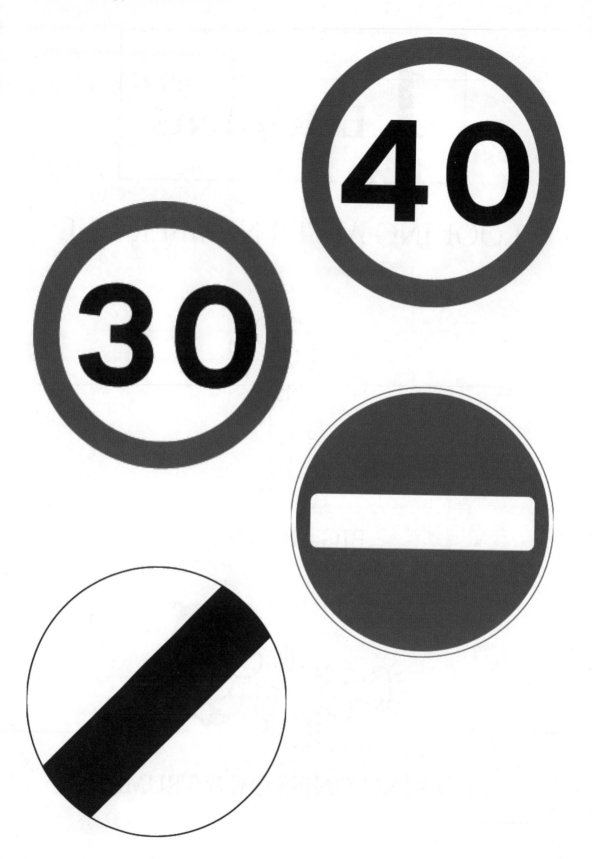

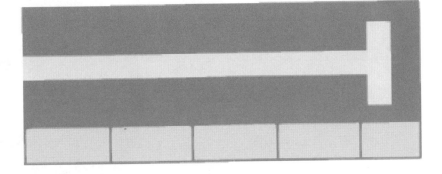

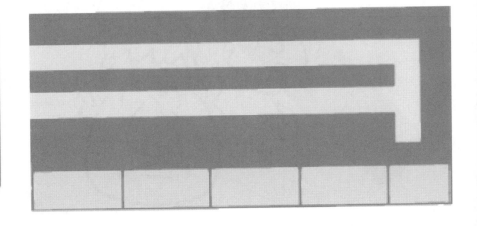

Down in the mouth

Down in the dumps

As miserable as sin

Raising a smile

As happy as Larry

Jesus heals the paralysed man

Jesus heals Legion

Jesus ministers to Martha and Mary